Best of
McCall's QUILTING

Fresh & Fun Appliqué

12 exciting patterns from the pages of *McCall's Quilting* make lovely appliqué achievable for any quilter. Quilts range from small to large and cute to classic, with bonus dimensional and embellishment techniques. Unique projects from top designers, clear, complete instructions, and beautiful photography…it's appliqué, *McCall's Quilting* style!

LEISURE ARTS
the art of everyday living
www.leisurearts.com

Best of McCall's QUILTING

FRESH AND FUN APPLIQUÉ

EDITORIAL

Editor-in-Chief	**Beth Hayes**
Art Director	**Ellie Brown**
Senior Editor	**Kathryn Patterson**
Associate Editor	**Sherri Bain Driver**
Assistant Editor	**Erin Russek**
Web Editor	**Valerie Uland**
Administrative Editor	**Susan Zinanti**
Graphic Designers	**Karen Gillis Taylor**
	Tracee Doran
	Joyce Robinson
Photography Stylist	**Ashley Slupe**
Photographer	**Mellisa Karlin Mahoney**

CREATIVE CRAFTS GROUP, LLC

President & CEO	**Stephen J. Kent**
CFO	**Mark F. Arnett**
SVP, General Manager	**Tina Battock**
VP, Publishing Director	**Joel P. Toner**
SVP, Chief Marketing Officer	**Nicole McGuire**
VP, Production	**Barbara Schmitz**
Corporate Controller	**Jordan Bohrer**
Product & Video Development	**Kristi Loeffelholz**

OPERATIONS

Circulation Director	**Deb Westmaas**
New Business Mgr.	**Lance Covert**
Renewal & Billing Mgr.	**Nekeya Dancy**
Newsstand Consultant	**T. J. Montilli**
Digital Marketing Mgr.	**Laurie Harris**
Online Subscription Mgr.	**Jodi Lee**
Director of IT	**Tom Judd**
Production Manager	**Dominic Taormina**
Ad Prod. Coordinator	**Sarah Katz**
Advertising Coordinator	**Madalene Becker**
Administrative Assistant	**Jane Flynn**
Retail Sales	**LaRita Godfrey, 800-815-3538**

ADVERTISING

Publisher	**Lisa O'Bryan, 303-215-5641**
Advertising	**Cristy Adamski, 715-824-4546**
Online Advertising	**Andrea Abrahamson, 303-215-5686**

EDITORIAL OFFICES

McCall's Quilting
741 Corporate Circle, Suite A, Golden, CO 80401
(303) 215-5600 (303) 215-5601 fax

Produced by the editors of
McCall's Quilting magazine
for
Leisure Arts, Inc.
5701 Ranch Drive, Little Rock, AR 72223-9633
www.leisurearts.com.
Library of Congress Control Number: 2013937083
ISBN-13/EAN: 978-1-4647-0860-2

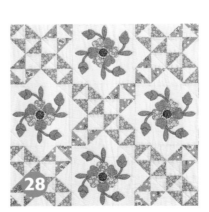

Contents

Buttons in Bloom

Designed by
ANN WEBER

SKILL LEVEL INTERMEDIATE

Finished Quilt Size
50" x 50"

Note: Appliqué templates are printed without seam allowance.

Number of Blocks and Finished Size
16 Checkerboard Blocks 10⅝" x 10⅝"

Fabric Requirements

Turquoise dot, aqua/green leaf print, **and** aqua floral (blocks)	⅝ yd. **each**
Gray dot (blocks, border)	⅞ yd.
White-on-white print (blocks)	1 yd.
Green swirl print (vine)	1 fat quarter*
Assorted green mottles/ prints (leaves)	½-⅝ yd. **total**
4 assorted orange prints (flowers)	¼ yd. **each**
2 assorted brown prints (flower centers)	7" x 7" piece **each**
Turquoise/blue large print (border)	½ yd.
Green/white check (bias-cut binding)	⅞ yd.
Backing	3⅜ yds.
Batting size	58" x 58"

*A fat quarter is an 18" x 20-22" cut of fabric.

Other Materials
48 assorted brown/tan buttons, 5/16"–½"
Bias bar, ½" (optional)

Photographed at Old Glory Antiques, 6851 S. Gaylord Street #239, Centennial, CO 80122; 303-798-4212; oldgloryantiquesinc.com.

Brighten a corner with this cheerful throw, and compliments are sure to follow. It's a quilt that's homey enough for comfort, yet distinctive enough to be truly memorable.

Planning

This cool quilt features fun pieced blocks and easy appliqué. Some of the stems of the leaves are longer than others depending on placement under the vines. Ann chose 2-holed buttons of various sizes and shades to embellish her flower centers.

Cutting Instructions

(cut in order listed)
Note: Cutting instructions for appliqué shapes are on templates.
⊠ = cut in half twice diagonally
◹ = cut in half diagonally
Turquoise dot
   6 strips 3" x width of fabric (WOF)
Aqua/green leaf print
   3 strips 3" x WOF
   6 strips 3" x 20"
Aqua floral
   6 strips 3" x 20"
   32 squares 3" x 3"
Gray dot
   3 strips 3" x 20"
   24 squares 5" x 5" ⊠
   8 squares 3" x 3" ◹
White-on-white print
   32 squares 5" x 5" ⊠
   32 squares 3" x 3" ◹
Green swirl print
   1 square 17" x 17" (for 136" of 1½"-wide
     bias-cut strip*)
Turquoise/blue large print
   52 squares 3" x 3"
Green/white check
   1 square 25" x 25" (for 2½"-wide
     bias-cut binding*)
*For help making continuous bias from a square, see **How to Make Continuous Bias**, pages 62-63.

Piecing the Blocks

1 Referring to **Diagram I-A**, sew together 2 turquoise dot and 1 aqua/green leaf WOF strips to make strip set. Make 3. Press in direction of arrows. Cut into 32 segments 3" wide.

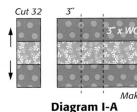

Cut 32   3"

3" x WOF

Make 3

Diagram I-A

In similar manner, make strip sets and cut segments as in **Diagram I-B**.

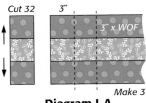

Cut 32 3″ 3″ x WOF Make 3

Diagram I-A

2 **Note:** The triangles on all edges and corners of blocks are cut oversized for subsequent trimming. Referring to **Diagram II-A**, arrange and sew 5 diagonal rows using 8 white-on-white print 5″ quarter-square triangles, 2 aqua floral 3″ squares, 2 short segments, and 1 long segment. Sew rows together.

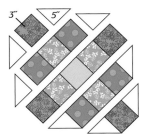

3″ 5″

Diagram II-A

Add white 3″ half-square triangles to corners (**Diagram II-B**).

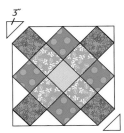

3″

Diagram II-B

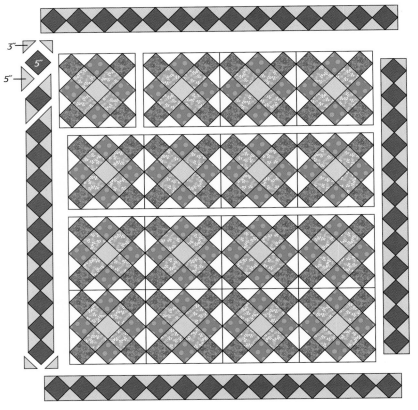

Assembly Diagram

Trim block to 11⅛″ square, centering (**Diagram II-C**). Make 16 Checkerboard Blocks.

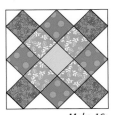

Make 16;
trim to 11⅛″ square
Diagram II-C

Assembling and Appliquéing the Quilt Top

3 **Note:** Refer to **Assembly Diagram** for following steps. Sew 4 rows of 4 blocks each. Sew rows together.

4 For side border strip, stitch together 22 gray 5″ quarter-square triangles and 12 turquoise/blue large print 3″ squares. Add gray 3″ half-square triangles to corners.

Trim edges even, ¼″ outside corners of squares. Make 2; sew to sides. For top/bottom border strip, stitch together 26 gray quarter-square triangles and 14 turquoise/blue squares. Add gray half-square triangles to corners. **Trim** edges even. Make 2; sew to top and bottom.

5 Referring to **Diagram III**, fold green swirl print 1½″ x 136″ bias-cut strip in half, wrong sides together. Stitch ½″ from fold. Trim seam allowance to ⅛″. Press tube flat, centering seam allowance on back so raw edge isn't visible from front. Using ½″ bias bar makes pressing faster and easier. From prepared tube, cut 4 vines each 34″.

½″

Diagram III

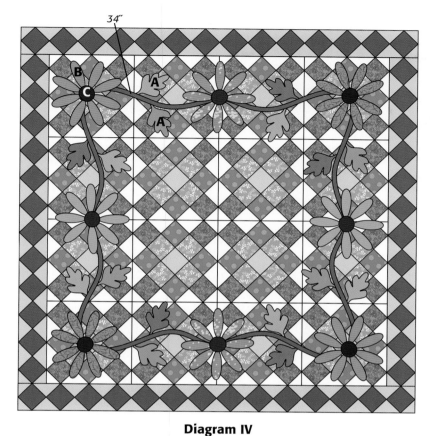

Diagram IV

6 Referring to **Diagram IV**, position leaves, vines, petals, and flower centers, using block seams as placement guide. Appliqué in place.

Quilting and Finishing

7 Layer, baste, and quilt. Ann machine outline quilted the appliqué. The 4 center blocks are quilted with straight-line grids and curves on the center squares. Border patches are stitched in the ditch.

8 Tack 6 assorted shades and sizes of buttons to each flower center. Bind quilt with bias-cut green/white check.

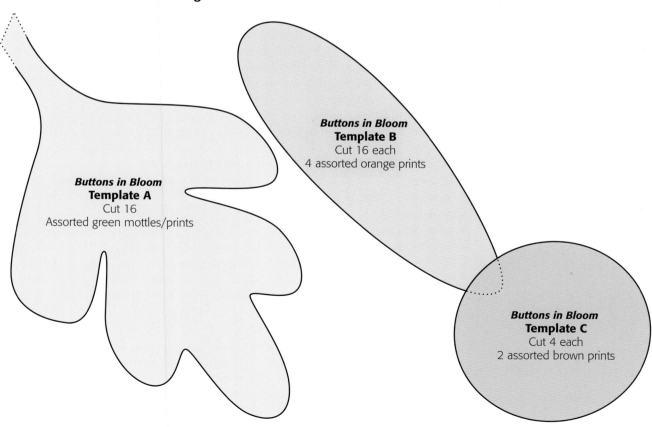

Buttons in Bloom
Template A
Cut 16
Assorted green mottles/prints

Buttons in Bloom
Template B
Cut 16 each
4 assorted orange prints

Buttons in Bloom
Template C
Cut 4 each
2 assorted brown prints

Bugs in My Posies

Designed by
HOLLY J. HOUSER

Machine Quilted by
DIANA JOHNSON

Add a playful touch of nature to a table or wall with this sweet summery design. It's **as much fun to make as it is to display.**

SKILL LEVEL **CONFIDENT BEGINNER**

Finished Wall Hanging Size
20½" x 36½"

Note: Appliqué templates are printed without seam allowance.

Number of Blocks and Finished Sizes
17 Appliquéd Blocks, assorted sizes

Fabric Requirements

Assorted light/medium green prints (blocks, border piecing)	1¼-1¾ yds. **total**
Assorted orange prints (flowers)	¼-⅜ yd. **total**
Assorted red prints (flowers)	⅜-½ yd. **total**
Dark green print (blocks)	11" x 11" piece
Assorted yellow prints (flowers)	¼-⅜ yd. **total**
Black solid (bugs)	7" x 8" piece
Red/black dot (bugs)	8" x 9" piece
White/black dot **and** black/white dot (flower centers)	6" x 6" piece **each**
White/green leaf print (blocks)	¼ yd.
Dark green mottle (leaves, vines)	¼ yd.
Black/white print (inner border)	¼ yd.
Green-on-green print (binding)	½ yd.
Paper-backed fusible web (optional)	1½ yds.
Backing	1⅜ yds.
Batting size	28" x 44"

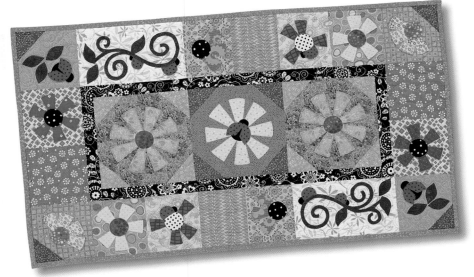

Planning

This little quilt is cute as a bug's ear! Trace and cut your template shapes casually, varying each just a bit, if you want to duplicate the relaxed look of Holly's appliqué. For fusible web appliqué methods, remember to reverse asymmetrical templates before use.

Holly fused her appliqué and then secured with machine straight stitch. She placed her pairs of matching blocks symmetrically in the quilt; do likewise if you wish.

Cutting Instructions
(cut in order listed)
Note: Cutting instructions for appliqué shapes are on templates.
Assorted light/medium green prints
    for corners of 2 large blocks, cut:
      8 matching squares 3" x 3"
    for large block backgrounds, cut:
      2 matching squares 8½" x 8½"
      1 square 8½" x 8½"
    for small block backgrounds, cut:
      2 sets of 2 matching rectangles
        5" x 5½"
      2 matching rectangles 4½" x 5½"
      3 sets of 2 matching
        squares 5½" x 5½"
    for border piecing, cut:
      2 matching rectangles 4½" x 5½"
      2 matching squares 5½" x 5½"
Dark green print
    8 squares 3" x 3"
White/green leaf print
    2 rectangles 5½" x 9½"
Black/white print
    *2 strips 1½" x 24½"
    *2 strips 1½" x 10½"
Green-on-green print
    4 strips 2½" x width of fabric
      (binding)
*Border strips are cut to exact length.

Making the Blocks

1 Draw diagonal line on wrong side of assorted light/medium green print 3" square. Place marked square on corner of 1 of 2 matching green 8½" squares (**Diagram I**), right sides together and aligning raw edges. Sew on marked line; trim away and discard excess fabric. Open and press. Repeat on all corners to make large pieced square. Make 2. Finger-press in half on both length and width; use folds as placement guide. Position A and B shapes as shown; appliqué in place. Make 2.

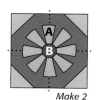

Make 2
Diagram I

2 Using Step 1 process, add dark green 3" squares to corners of remaining green 8½" square (**Diagram II**). Finger-press, position A, C, and D shapes, and appliqué.

Make 1
Diagram II

3 In similar manner, make 14 assorted small blocks as shown in **Diagrams III** through **IX**.

4 Sew together 3 large blocks to make quilt center. Sew black/white print 24½″ strips to long sides. Sew black/white 10½″ strips to short sides.

5 To make long border, stitch together 4 small blocks and 4½″ x 5½″ green rectangle as shown. Make 2. Sew to long sides.

Stitch together 3 small blocks and green 5½″ square to make short border. Make 2. Sew to short sides.

Quilting and Finishing

6 Layer, baste, and quilt. Diana machine outline quilted the appliqué and quilted a swirling design in all green background areas. The inner border features a looping line. Bind with green-on-green print.

5″ x 5½″
Diagram III
Make 2

5″ x 5½″
E G
B F
Diagram IV
Make 2

4½″ x 5½″
E
B
Diagram V
Make 2

5½″ x 9½″
F
K G
I
H
Diagram VI
Make 2

3″ 5½″
B
L
Diagram VII
Make 2

5½″
E
B
Diagram VIII
Make 2 total

5½″ 3″
D J
C
Diagram IX
Make 2

Assembling the Quilt Top
Note: Refer to **Assembly Diagram** for following steps.

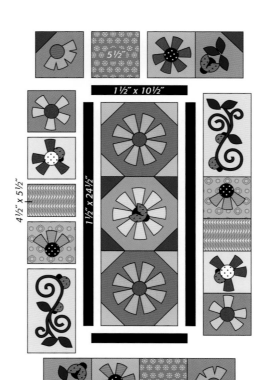

1½″ x 10½″
1½″ x 24½″
4½″ x 5½″
5½″ x 5½″

Assembly Diagram

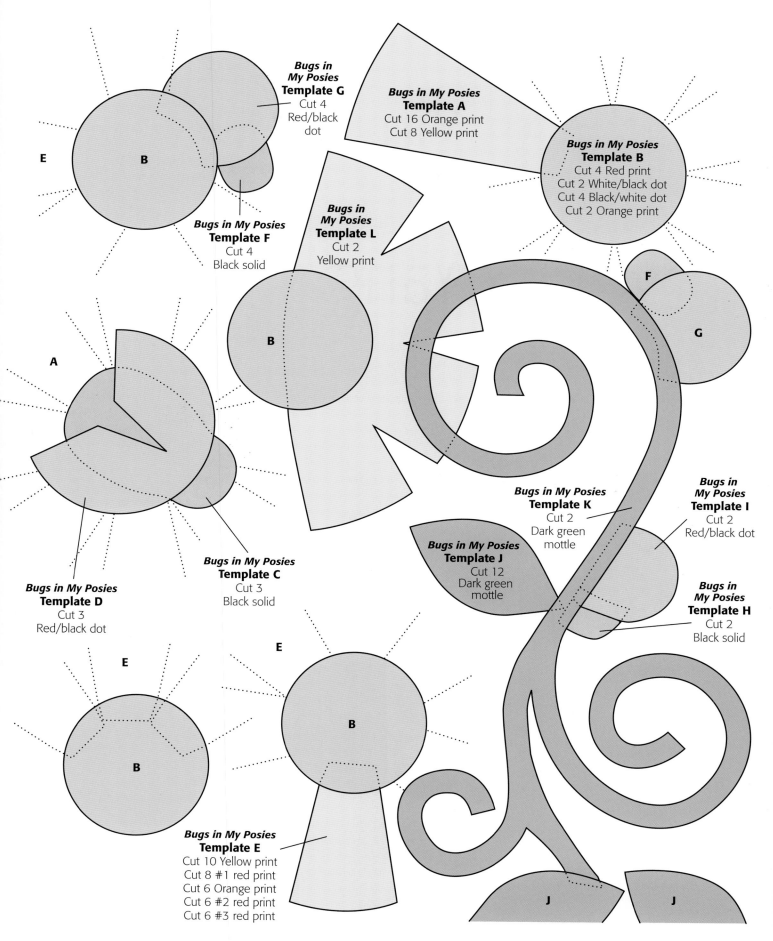

Bugs in My Posies
Template G
Cut 4
Red/black dot

Bugs in My Posies
Template A
Cut 16 Orange print
Cut 8 Yellow print

Bugs in My Posies
Template B
Cut 4 Red print
Cut 2 White/black dot
Cut 4 Black/white dot
Cut 2 Orange print

E

B

Bugs in My Posies
Template F
Cut 4
Black solid

Bugs in My Posies
Template L
Cut 2
Yellow print

B

F

G

A

B

Bugs in My Posies
Template K
Cut 2
Dark green
mottle

Bugs in My Posies
Template I
Cut 2
Red/black dot

Bugs in My Posies
Template J
Cut 12
Dark green
mottle

Bugs in My Posies
Template H
Cut 2
Black solid

Bugs in My Posies
Template D
Cut 3
Red/black dot

Bugs in My Posies
Template C
Cut 3
Black solid

E

E

B

B

Bugs in My Posies
Template E
Cut 10 Yellow print
Cut 8 #1 red print
Cut 6 Orange print
Cut 6 #2 red print
Cut 6 #3 red print

J

J

Designed by
TOBY LISCHKO

Yin and Yang

Dark and light…male and female…these are only a few of the seemingly contrary forces interwoven in the natural world. Make this quilt as a celebration of life's dualities, or simply for its graphic power.

SKILL LEVEL **INTERMEDIATE**

Finished Quilt Size
65½" x 78½"

Note: Template A is oversized to allow for subsequent trimming of block. Appliqué Template D is printed without seam allowance.

Number of Blocks and Finished Size
20 Yin and Yang Blocks 12" x 12"

Fabric Requirements

Black/taupe leaf print (blocks, sashing posts, border)	2⅜ yds.
Cream/taupe dot, black/gray texture, cream/taupe/black print, black/cream dot, cream/taupe texture, gray/black texture, **and** cream/gray leaf print (blocks)	1 yd. **each**
Gray/taupe stripe (sashing, binding)	1⅝ yds.
Backing (piece lengthwise)	5 yds.
Batting size	74" x 88"

Other Materials
Template plastic
Super-fine pins (0.4mm), optional*
*Toby prefers to use super-fine pins when pinning curves.

Photographed at Scandinavian Designs, 9000 E. Hampden Ave., Denver, CO 80231; www.ScandinavianDesigns.com.

Planning

Toby's easy pinning and sewing techniques take the fear out of curved piecing in this dynamic quilt.

Cutting Instructions*
(cut in order listed)

Black/taupe leaf print
  **4 strips 6½" x 70", cut on lengthwise grain
  10 Template A
  5 **each** Templates B, C, **and** D
  30 squares 1½" x 1½"

Cream/taupe dot, black/gray texture, cream/taupe/black print, black/cream dot, cream/taupe texture, gray/black texture, **and** cream/gray leaf print—**cut from each:**
  10 Template A
  5 **each** Templates B, C, **and** D
Gray/taupe stripe
  8 strips 2½" x width of fabric (binding)
  49 strips 1½" x 12½"

*See **Cutting the Template Shapes** on the next page before cutting.
**Border strips include extra length for trimming.

Cutting the Template Shapes

1 Trace Template A-D shapes, including grain lines and match points, on template plastic. Cut out, and make holes at match points using a stiletto or large needle. Watching grain lines, place templates **right** side down on **wrong** sides of appropriate fabrics. Trace around, cut out shapes, and mark match points on wrong side of each shape.

Pinning and Stitching Curves and Blocks

Note: Instructions are for 1 block; repeat to make 20 blocks total. Each block uses 2 Template A, 1 Template B, 1 Template C, and 1 Template D **each** of 2 fabrics (1 light and 1 dark).

2 Lay out all pieces for one block (**Photo A**).

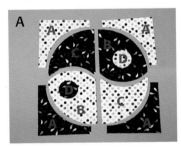

With right sides together and C on top, pin contrasting B and C shapes together along short curves as follows. Aligning edges at seam ends and with head of pin away from seam, weave a pin through both layers, parallel to aligned edges (**Photo B**). Repeat at opposite end of seam.

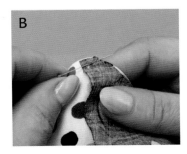

3 At end of curve where seam is to finish, insert another pin, perpendicular to pin already in place, and parallel to seam

(**Photo C**). This pin will be removed as seam is stitched.

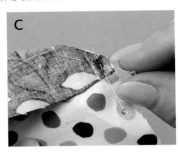

Align match points and insert final pin (**Photo D**) at middle of curve.

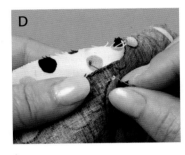

4 Set sewing machine needle to the furthest right position possible. Lower needle onto ¼" line on ruler, align straight edge of a small piece of adhesive foam (Toby uses Dr. Scholl's® Molefoam® Padding) with ruler and adhere to machine (**Photo E**). Adhesive foam should be parallel to sewing foot.

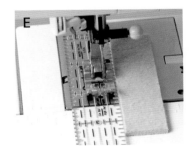

Making sure that raw edges of fabric always touch the foam and stitching slowly, take 2-3 stitches at the beginning of the seam (**Photo F**).

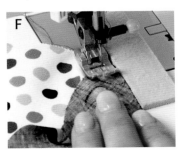

With needle down and referring to **Photo G**, hold the center pin and give the fabric a slight tug, just enough to align curved edges. (**Hint:** A stiletto may be helpful when aligning edges.) Manipulating fabric edges to meet, stitch to center, removing pin as you approach, and stop with needle down.

Hold pinned end and give fabric a slight tug as before, again manipulating fabric edges to meet (**Photo H**).

Sew until close to pin now pointing to the foot. Holding pin down with finger, continue to stitch slowly, easing pin out of fabric as you sew (**Photo I**).

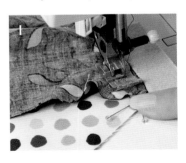

Referring to **Photo J**, use last pin to keep edge of curve in contact with foam until seam is complete. Press seam toward B.

5 In same manner, stitch together remaining B and C shapes for first block.

6 Referring to **Photo K**, stitch 2 A/A units as shown.

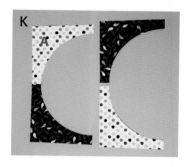

7 Make a mark on curved B/C seam, ¼″ in from curved edge (**Photo L**).

Pin A/A to B/C, aligning seam of A/A with seam of B/C at marked point (**Photo M**).

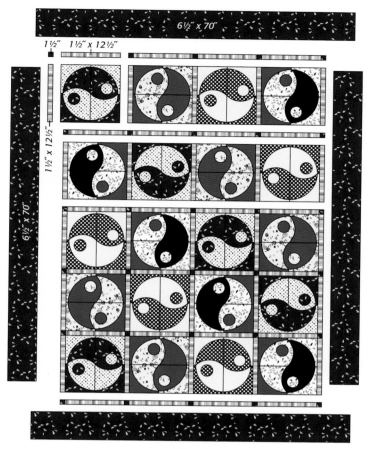

Assembly Diagram

Stitch together, using Steps 2-4 technique, to make block half. Repeat with remaining A/A and B/C units to make remaining block half.

8 Use Step 7 technique to mark curved seams ¼″ in from inner edges of block halves. Stitch block halves together (**Photo N**), aligning marks. Aligning match points on Template B and D shapes, position and appliqué D shapes in place. To complete Yin and Yang Block, **trim** block to 12½″ x 12½″, centering design. Make 20 blocks total (5 of each fabric combination).

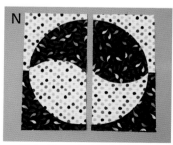

Make 20 total; trim to 12½″ square after appliqué.

Quilt Top Assembly

Note: Refer to **Assembly Diagram** for following steps.

9 Stitch 6 sashing rows using 5 black leaf 1½″ squares and 4 stripe 12½″ sashing strips each. Referring to photo (page 12) for block placement and orientation, sew 5 block rows of 5 sashing strips and 4 blocks each. Sew rows together, alternating.

10 Sew black leaf 70″ strips to sides; trim even with top and bottom. Sew remaining 70″ strips to top/bottom; trim even with sides.

Quilting and Finishing

11 Layer, baste, and quilt. Toby used Fairfield Bamboo batting. She machine quilted feathers in the B/C shapes and a large teardrop in each A shape. The sashing strips are quilted in the ditch and the outer border features a meandering feather design. Bind with gray/taupe stripe.

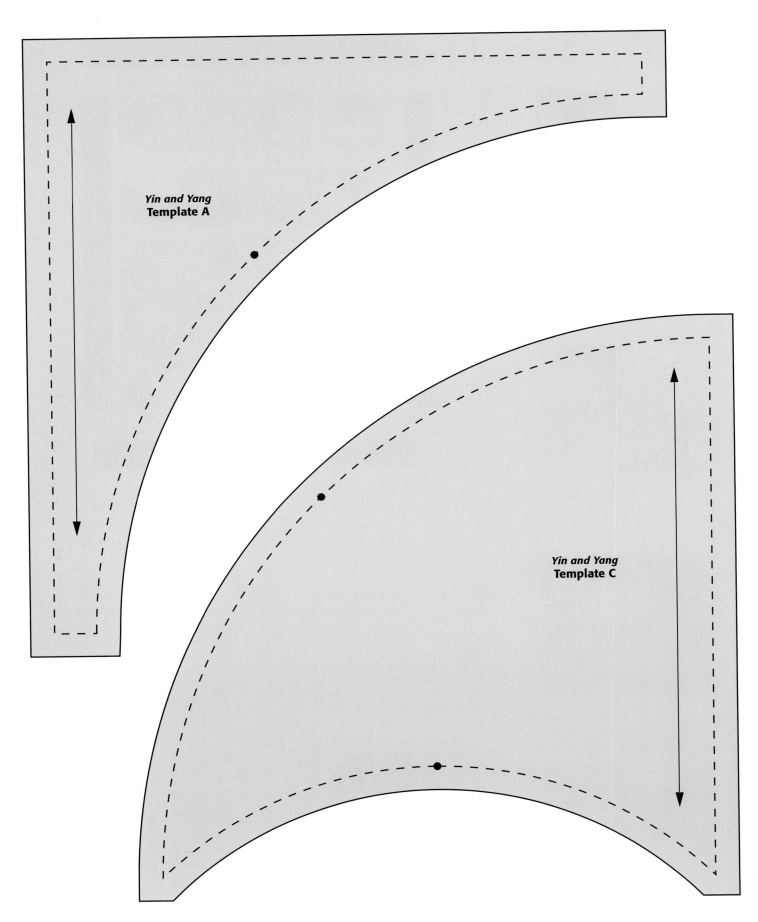

Yin and Yang
Template A

Yin and Yang
Template C

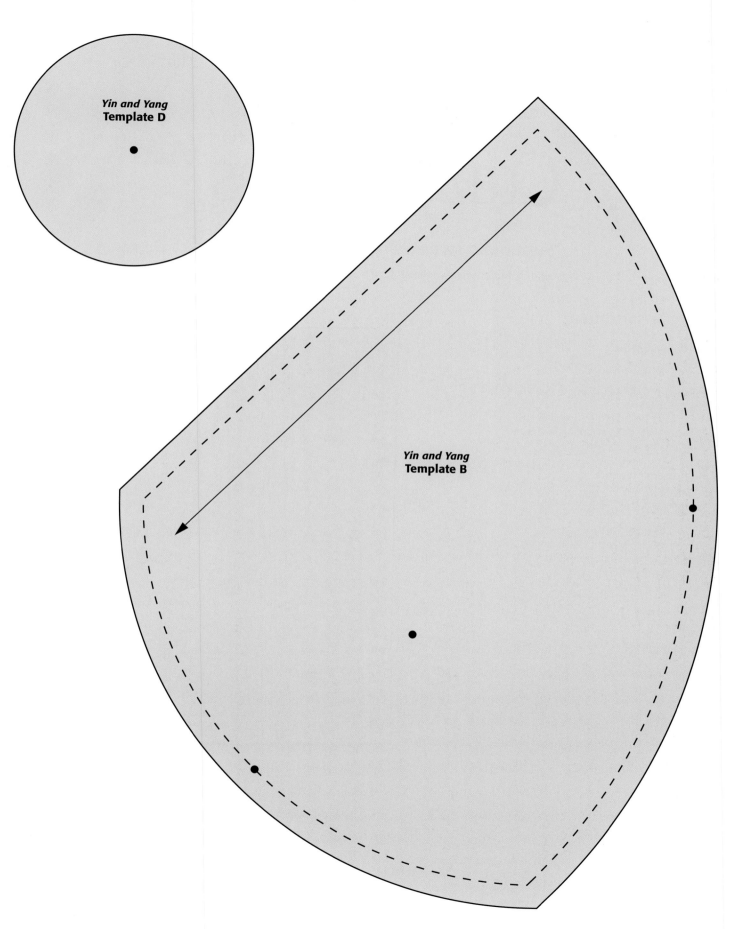

Yin and Yang
Template D

Yin and Yang
Template B

Crazy Dazies

Summer's sweetest quilt features tilted blocks, 1930s repro prints, and a meadow's worth of bright bugs against a crisp white background. You'll love using it all year long!

SKILL LEVEL **INTERMEDIATE**

Finished Quilt Size
73" x 83"

Note: Appliqué templates are printed without seam allowance.

Number of Blocks and Finished Size
42 Daisy Blocks 10" x 10"

Fabric Requirements

White-on-white print (blocks, outer border)	3⅛ yds.
Assorted prints (appliqué, blocks)	3¾-4¼ yds. **total***
Yellow small floral (daisy centers)	¼ yd.
Cream/multicolor print (block backgrounds)	5⅜ yds.
Blue/white print (inner border)	⅝ yd.
Green print (stems)	⅜ yd.
Black solid (ladybugs)	9" x 10" piece
Red print (ladybug wings)	10" x 13" piece
Light blue dot **and** yellow solid (bees)	4" x 5" piece **each**
Black/multicolor print (binding)	⅞ yd.
Backing (piece lengthwise)	5¼ yds.
Batting size	82" x 92"

Square acrylic ruler, 12" or larger
Bias bar, ½" (optional)
Embroidery floss, black and colors to accent butterfly wings
*See **Planning**.

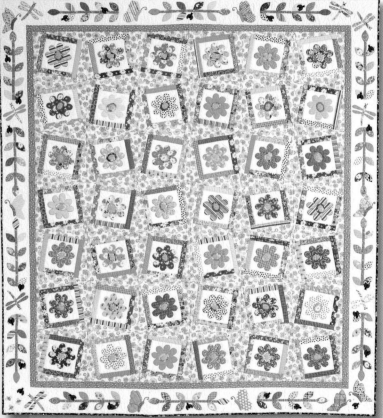

Cutting Instructions
(cut in order listed)
Note: Cutting instructions for appliqué shapes are on templates.

White-on-white print
*4 strips 5½" x 78", cut on lengthwise grain
42 squares 7" x 7"
Assorted prints—**cut a total of:**
84 strips 1½" x 8½"
84 strips 1½" x 6½"

Cream/multicolor print
84 strips 3½" x 14½"
84 strips 3½" x 8½"
Blue/white print
*4 strips 1¾" x 74", pieced from 8 width of fabric (WOF) strips

Green print
14 strips 1½" x 12"
Black/multicolor print
9 strips 2½" x WOF (binding)
*Border strips include extra length for trimming.

Designed by
AUDREY HIERS

Planning

Audrey used forty-two 10″ squares from a 1930s repro print Layer Cake™ precut fabric pack, a coordinating Charm Pack of 5″ squares, and a few scraps from her stash for her assorted prints. Blocks are made oversized, then trimmed to tilt; our photos on page 20 show you how.

Two of the Template B shapes were fussy-cut centered on printed flowers, and Template C centers were omitted for those daisies. Daisies and other appliqué shapes were placed casually, many off-center, for a fun, whimsical look. Audrey positioned an assorted green Template D leaf at each stem end. Do likewise if you wish.

Making the Blocks

① Finger-press white-on-white print 7″ square in half on both length and width; use folds as placement guide. Referring to **Diagram I**, position A–C in alphabetical order.

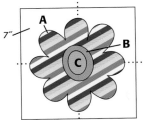

Diagram I

Make 42 total; trim to 6½″ square

Appliqué in place. Finish appliqué edges with machine blanket stitch (**Diagram II**) if desired. **Trim** appliquéd square to 6½″ square. Make 42 total.

Diagram II

② Sew assorted 6½″ strips to top and bottom of trimmed square (**Diagram III**). Stitch assorted 8½″ strips to sides. Sew cream/multicolor print 8½″ strips to top/bottom. Sew cream/multicolor 14½″ strips to sides to make Daisy Block. Make 42 total.

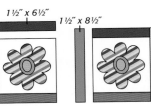
1½″ x 6½″

1½″ x 8½″

3½″ x 8½″

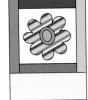

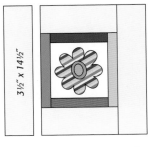

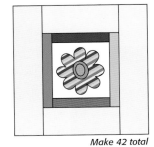

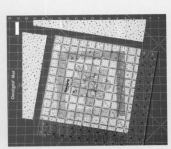
3½″ x 14½″

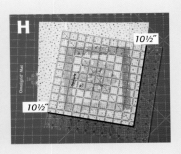

Make 42 total

Diagram III

Trimming the Blocks

③ Position square acrylic ruler so 10½″ perpendicular lines on ruler are within block and remaining 2 edges of ruler are also within block (**photo A**).

Trim 2 sides of block (**photo B**).

④ Rotate block (**photo C**), align 10½″ lines with cut edges, and **trim** remaining 2 edges to complete block (**photo D**).

Repeat to trim 21 total blocks in same orientation (**photo E**).

⑤ Referring to **photos F–J**, reverse orientation to trim 21 remaining blocks.

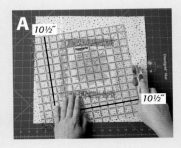
A 10½″ 10½″

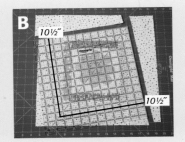
B 10½″ 10½″

E Trim 21 total

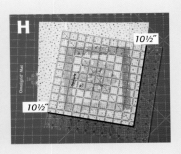
H 10½″ 10½″

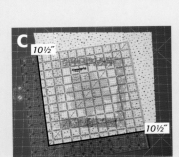
C 10½″ 10½″

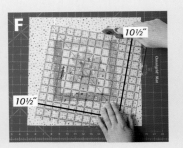
F 10½″ 10½″

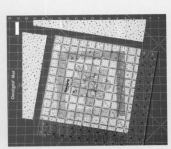
I

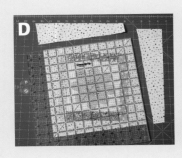
D

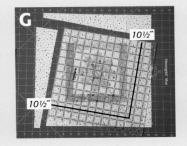
G 10½″ 10½″

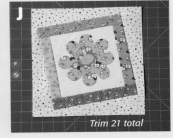
J Trim 21 total

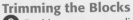

5½" x 78"

1¾" x 74"

5½" x 78"

1¾" x 74"

Assembly Diagram

Assembling and Appliquéing the Quilt Top

Note: Refer to **Assembly Diagram** for following steps.

6 Sew 7 rows of 6 trimmed blocks each, alternating orientation. Sew rows together.

7 Stitch blue/white print 74" strips to sides; trim even with top and bottom. Stitch remaining 74" strips to top/bottom; trim even with sides. Sew white 78" strips to sides; trim even. Sew remaining 78" strips to top/bottom; trim even.

8 Fold green print 1½" x 12" strip in half lengthwise, wrong sides together (**Diagram IV**). Stitch ½" from fold. **Trim** seam allowance to ⅛". Press tube flat, centering seam allowance on back so raw edge isn't visible from front. Using ½" bias bar makes pressing easier. Make 14 stems.

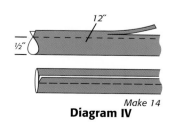

12"

½"

Make 14

Diagram IV

French Knot

Straight Stitch

Stem Stitch

Diagram VI

Diagram V

9 Referring to **Diagram V** and **photos**, position stems and D-O on white border strips, tucking under ends of stems not covered by leaves. Appliqué in place. Blanket-stitch edges if desired. Use 2 strands of embroidery floss and stitches shown in **Diagram VI** to add details to assorted bugs (see **templates** for placement).

Quilting and Finishing
10 Layer, baste, and quilt. Audrey machine quilted blocks and borders in the ditch. She outline quilted the appliqué, and filled the outer border with a meander. Bind with black/multicolor print.

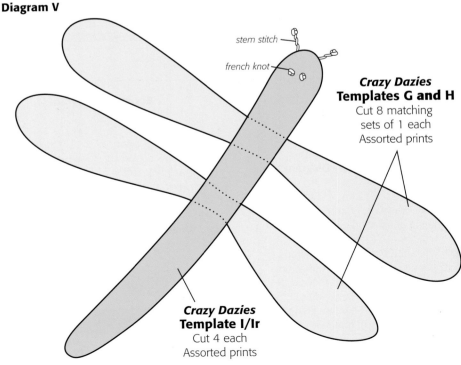

stem stitch

french knot

Crazy Dazies
Templates G and H
Cut 8 matching sets of 1 each
Assorted prints

Crazy Dazies
Template I/Ir
Cut 4 each
Assorted prints

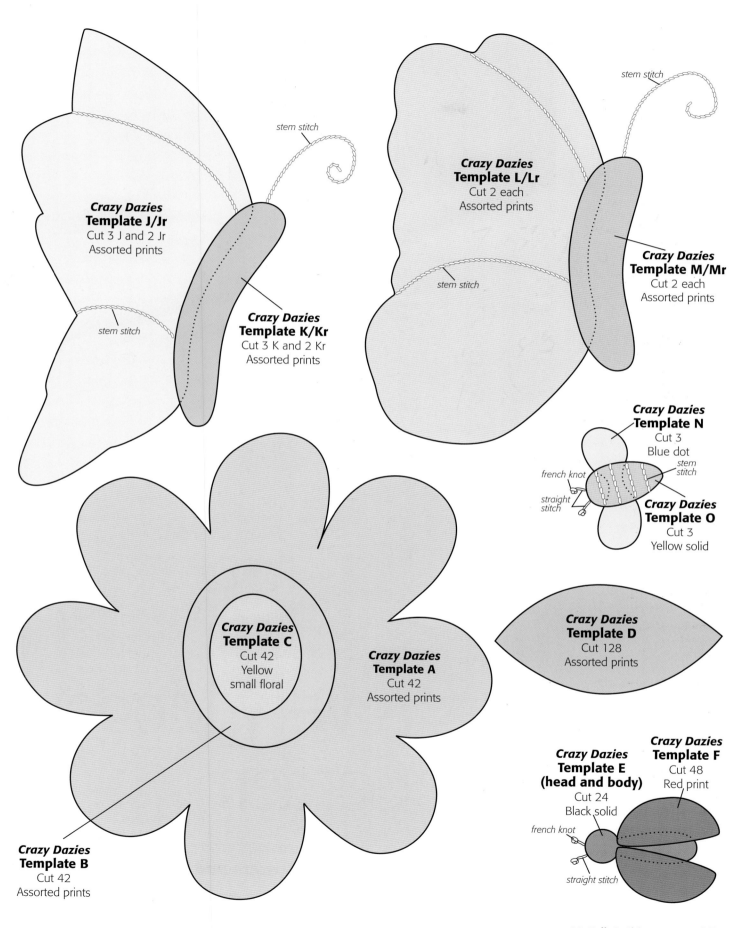

Crazy Dazies
Template J/Jr
Cut 3 J and 2 Jr
Assorted prints

stem stitch

stem stitch

Crazy Dazies
Template K/Kr
Cut 3 K and 2 Kr
Assorted prints

Crazy Dazies
Template L/Lr
Cut 2 each
Assorted prints

stem stitch

stem stitch

Crazy Dazies
Template M/Mr
Cut 2 each
Assorted prints

Crazy Dazies
Template N
Cut 3
Blue dot

french knot

stem stitch

straight stitch

Crazy Dazies
Template O
Cut 3
Yellow solid

Crazy Dazies
Template C
Cut 42
Yellow
small floral

Crazy Dazies
Template A
Cut 42
Assorted prints

Crazy Dazies
Template D
Cut 128
Assorted prints

Crazy Dazies
Template B
Cut 42
Assorted prints

Crazy Dazies
**Template E
(head and body)**
Cut 24
Black solid

Crazy Dazies
Template F
Cut 48
Red print

french knot

straight stitch

Designed by
DOROTHY ANN WELD

Made by
DOROTHY ANN WELD
and JUDY HART

Machine Quilted by
LOUISE D. SMITH

SKILL LEVEL
CONFIDENT BEGINNER

Finished Quilt Size
84½" x 84½"

Note: Flower templates
are printed with
seam allowance.

**Number of Blocks
and Finished Size**
16 Pieced Blocks 12" x 12"

Fabric Requirements

Light pink texture (blocks)	1 yd.
Green/pink large floral (blocks, border)	2½ yds.
Green texture (blocks, border, leaves)	3 yds.
Yellow dot (blocks, border, flower centers)	1¼ yds.
Pink dot (blocks, border, petals, binding)	3⅜ yds.
White/multicolor print (squares)	1⅞ yds.
Template plastic	7" x 14" piece
Backing	7⅞ yds.
Batting size	94" x 110"*

*Includes batting for dimensional flowers.
See **Growing a Garden**, on the next page.

A Very Modern Garden

Sweet floral fabrics come to life with the addition of **easy dimensional flowers and leaves**. Photos walk you through construction, step by step.

Piecing the Blocks

1 Mark an accurate 6⅝″ x 13¼″ rectangle on template plastic (**Diagram I**). Cut out rectangle directly on marked lines. Make a mark at the midpoint (6⅝″) of 1 long side. Mark lines connecting the midpoint with the opposite corners of the rectangle. Cut directly on the 2 angled lines to make large triangle template.

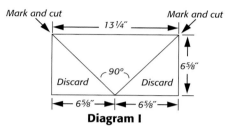

Diagram I

2 Referring to **Diagram II-A**, sew light pink and green texture WOF strips to sides of green/pink large floral WOF **or** 40″ strip to make strip set. Press seams in direction of arrow. Make 12. Place plastic triangle template on strip set, aligning long template edge with raw edge of strip set. Tip of template will extend about ⅛″ beyond opposite raw edge of strip set. Mark along angled sides. Using rotary cutter and acrylic ruler, cut directly on marked lines to make large triangle. Rotate template and repeat mark and cut process to make 2nd large triangle. Cut 4 large triangles from each strip set.

In same manner, make and cut 4 strip sets as shown in **Diagram II-B**. **Note:** Handle bias edges of triangles carefully to avoid distortion. Using spray starch when pressing strip sets can help stabilize fabric.

3 Stitch together 4 large triangles cut from Diagram II-A strip set, 2 of each arrangement, to make Pieced Block (**Diagram III-A**). Make 12 for quilt center.

Growing a Garden

Dimensional flowers add a fun touch of whimsy; our photos beginning on the next page show you how. Choose a low-loft batting for best results with the 3-D technique.

Cutting Instructions

(cut first and in order listed)
Note: Cutting instructions for flower shapes are on templates.
Light pink texture
   12 strips 2½″ x width of fabric (WOF)
Green/pink large floral
   *4 strips 6½″ x 64″, cut on lengthwise grain
   5 strips 2½″ x 40″, cut on lengthwise grain
   7 strips 2½″ x WOF
Green texture
   *4 strips 2½″ x 64″, pieced from 8 WOF strips
   16 strips 2½″ x WOF
Yellow dot
   *4 strips 2½″ x 64″, pieced from 8 WOF strips
   4 strips 2½″ x WOF

Pink dot
   10 strips 2½″ x WOF (binding)
   *4 strips 2½″ x 64″, pieced from 8 WOF strips
   4 strips 2½″ x WOF
White/multicolor print
   13 squares 12½″ x 12½″
Batting
   1 square 94″ x 94″
*Border strips include extra length for trimming.

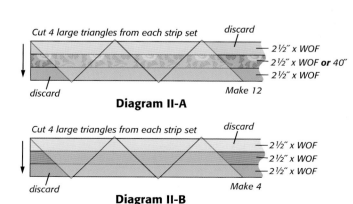

Cut 4 large triangles from each strip set   discard
   2½″ x WOF
   2½″ x WOF **or** 40″
   2½″ x WOF
discard   Make 12
Diagram II-A

Cut 4 large triangles from each strip set   discard
   2½″ x WOF
   2½″ x WOF
   2½″ x WOF
discard   Make 4
Diagram II-B

Make 12
Diagram III-A

Referring to **Diagram III-B**, make 4 blocks for border corners.

Make 4

Diagram III-B

Assembling the Quilt Top

Note: Refer to **Assembly Diagram** for following steps. Watch block placement and orientation.

④ Sew 3 rows of 3 white/multicolor print 12½" squares and 2 blocks each. Sew 2 rows of 3 blocks and 2 white squares each. Sew rows together, alternating.

⑤ Stitch together 1 each green/pink large floral, yellow dot, pink dot, and green texture 64" strips. Make 4. Measure exact width of quilt center from raw edge to raw edge. **Trim** two 64" pieced strips to this measurement, and sew Pieced Blocks to ends, watching orientation. Stitch untrimmed pieced 64" strips to sides; trim even with top and bottom. Stitch pieced strips (with blocks) to top/bottom.

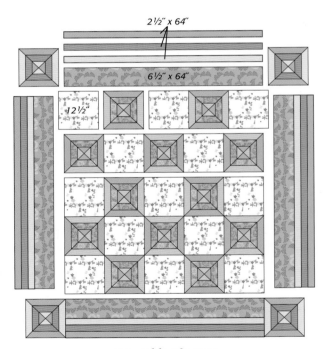

2½" x 64"

6½" x 64"

12½"

Assembly Diagram

Quilting and Binding

⑥ Layer, baste, and quilt. Louise used Warm & Natural® batting and machine quilted blocks and wide border strips in the ditch. She detail quilted the white squares and wide border strips. Flower motifs are stitched on blocks, and the narrow border strips feature a repeating feather motif. Bind with pink dot.

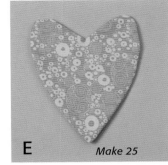

A

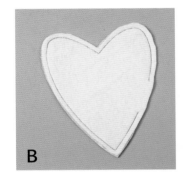

B

C

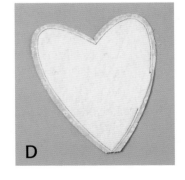

D

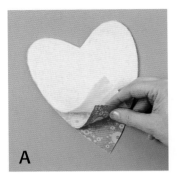

E   *Make 25*

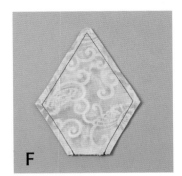

F

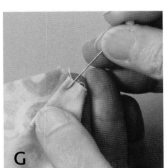

G

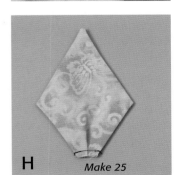

H   *Make 25*

Adding Dimensional Flowers

⑦ To make petal, layer 2 fabric As, right sides together, and 1 batting A (**photo A**).

Sew ¼" from raw edges through all layers, leaving an opening for turning (**photo B**). Clip just to stitching at petal indentation (**photo C**).

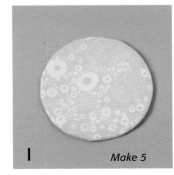

I   *Make 5*

J

K

L

M

Trim tip, and trim batting close to stitching (**photo D**).

Turn petal right side out; press. Hand stitch the opening closed. Make 25 (**photo E**).

8 To make leaf, sew 2 Bs right sides together, leaving flat end open (**photo F**).

Trim corners and turn right side out; press. Fold a small pleat at flat end, so bottom of leaf measures approximately ¾″ (**photo G**); pin.

Machine stitch ¼″ from raw edges, securing pleat (**photo H**). Make 25.

9 Make 5 flower centers, using Step 7 technique and C fabric and batting pieces (**photo I**).

10 Referring to quilt **photo** and using seams as placement guide, position 5 petals on quilt (**photo J**).

Blindstitch bottoms of petals to quilt top (**photo K**), 3½″ from tip along each side of each petal.

Position 5 leaves on petals (**photo L**); blindstitch short sides to petals. **Note:** Dorothy Ann used small pieces of Steam-A-Seam 2® fusible web to further secure petals and leaves; do likewise if you wish.

Position flower center (**photo M**); blindstitch in place. Repeat Step 10 to add 5 flowers total.

A Very Modern Garden
½ **Template A**
Cut 50
Pink dot
Cut 25
Batting

place on fold

A Very Modern Garden
½ **Template B**
Cut 50
Green texture

A Very Modern Garden
½ **Template C**
Cut 10
Yellow dot
Cut 5
Batting

place on fold

SKILL LEVEL **INTERMEDIATE**

Finished Quilt Size
55" x 55"

Note: Appliqué templates are printed without seam allowance.

Number of Blocks and Finished Size
13 Pierced Star Blocks 8" x 8"
12 Rose Blocks 8" x 8"

Fabric Requirements

Aqua small floral (Pierced Star Blocks)	½ yd.
Pink floral dot (Pierced Star Blocks)	⅜ yd.
Cream solid (blocks, 1st and 3rd borders)	2¼ yds.
Green print (leaves, stems)	½ yd.
White/red small print (buds, petals)	⅜ yd.
Pink small floral (petals, 2nd border)	⅝ yd.
White/red/pink print (flower centers)	⅛ yd.
Black small print (flower centers)	7" x 8" piece
Green large floral (4th border, binding)	1⅞ yds.
Backing	3⅝ yds.
Batting size	64" x 64"

Dainty Bess

Designed by
NANCY MAHONEY

Grandmother's garden bloomed with old-fashioned roses like these, and her quilts blossomed with fabric prints she'd recognize in these charming 30s repros. This tribute to a simpler time is perfect as both a decorating accent and a comforting nap quilt.

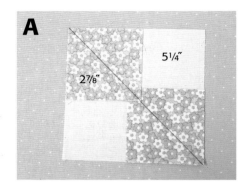

A

$2^{7/8}''$ $5^{1/4}''$

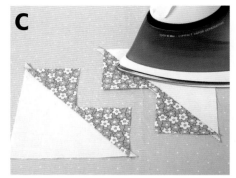

C

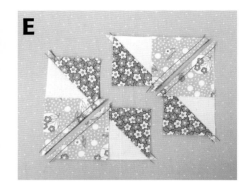

E

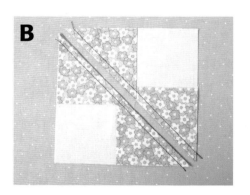

B

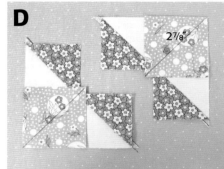

D

$2^{7/8}''$

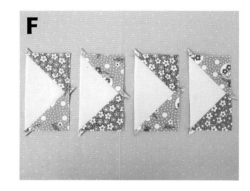

F

Planning

With 52 flying geese units to make, half with aqua triangles on the left and half with pink, the fast, no-waste technique shown in our photos will speed you through construction with complete accuracy.

Cutting Instructions
(cut in order listed)

Note: Cutting instructions for appliqué shapes are on templates.

Aqua small floral
   52 squares $2^{7/8}''$ x $2^{7/8}''$

Pink floral dot
   39 squares $2^{7/8}''$ x $2^{7/8}''$

Cream solid
   *4 strips $1^{1/4}''$ x 54", cut on lengthwise grain
   *4 strips 2" x 48", cut on lengthwise grain
   12 squares 9" x 9"
   13 squares $5^{1/4}''$ x $5^{1/4}''$
   39 squares $2^{7/8}''$ x $2^{7/8}''$
   26 squares $2^{1/2}''$ x $2^{1/2}''$

Pink small floral
   *4 strips $2^{1/2}''$ x 52", pieced from 6 width of fabric strips

Green large floral
   *4 strips $3^{1/2}''$ x 60", cut on lengthwise grain
   5 strips $2^{1/2}''$ x 50", cut on lengthwise grain (binding)

*Border strips include extra length for trimming.

No-Waste Flying Geese

1 Draw diagonal line on wrong side of each of 2 aqua small floral and 2 pink floral dot $2^{7/8}''$ squares. Place marked aqua squares on opposite corners of cream solid $5^{1/4}''$ square, right sides together and aligning raw edges (**photo A**).

Sew $^{1/4}''$ seam on each side of marked line; cut apart on marked line (**photo B**).

Open and press aqua triangles (**photo C**).

Place pink square on cream corner of each unit, right sides together (**photo D**).

Sew $^{1/4}''$ seam on each side of marked lines; cut apart on marked lines (**photo E**).

Open and press pink triangles to complete 4 flying geese units, 2 of each arrangement (**photo F**).

Repeat process to make 26 flying geese units of each arrangement (**Diagram I**).

Make 26   *Make 26*
Diagram I

Piecing and Appliquéing the Blocks

2 Draw diagonal line on wrong side of cream 2⅞″ square. Referring to **Diagram II-A**, place marked square on aqua 2⅞″ square, right sides together. Sew ¼″ seam on each side of marked line; cut apart on marked line. Open and press to make 2 pieced squares. Make 52.

Make 52

Diagram II-A

Repeat process using cream and pink floral dot 2⅞″ squares to make 26 pieced squares (**Diagram II-B**).

Make 26

Diagram II-B

Sew 2 cream/aqua pieced squares and 2 cream 2½″ squares together to make block center (**Diagram II-C**). Make 13.

Make 13

Diagram II-C

3 Referring to **Diagram III**, sew 3 rows using 4 pieced squares (2 of each color), 4 flying geese (2 of each arrangement), and block center. Sew rows together to make Pierced Star Block. Make 13.

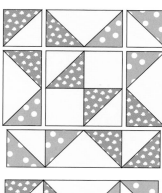

Make 13

Diagram III

4 Note: The cream appliqué background squares are cut oversized to allow for shrinkage during appliqué. Finger-press cream 9″ square in half on both length and width; use folds as placement guide. Referring to **Diagram IV**, position A-G in alphabetical order, keeping in mind that square will be trimmed to 8½″ x 8½″ (finished size is 8″ square). Appliqué in place. **Trim** to 8½″ square. Make 12 Rose Blocks.

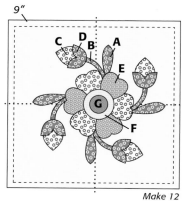

Make 12
Trim to 8½″ square

Diagram IV

Assembly Diagram

Assembling the Quilt Top

Note: Refer to **Assembly Diagram** for following steps.

5 Sew 5 rows of 5 blocks each, alternating. Sew rows together.

6 Stitch cream 48″ strips to sides; trim even with top and bottom. Stitch remaining cream 48″ strips to top/bottom; trim even with sides. In same manner, sew remaining borders to quilt, adding side strips first for each border and trimming even after each addition.

Quilting and Finishing

7 Layer, baste, and quilt. Nancy machine quilted diagonal lines across the Pierced Star Blocks, continuing across the corners of the Rose Blocks. She outline quilted the appliqué. Two straight lines are quilted on the 1st border, a curved line on the pink border, and a straight line with leaves on the green border. Bind with green large floral.

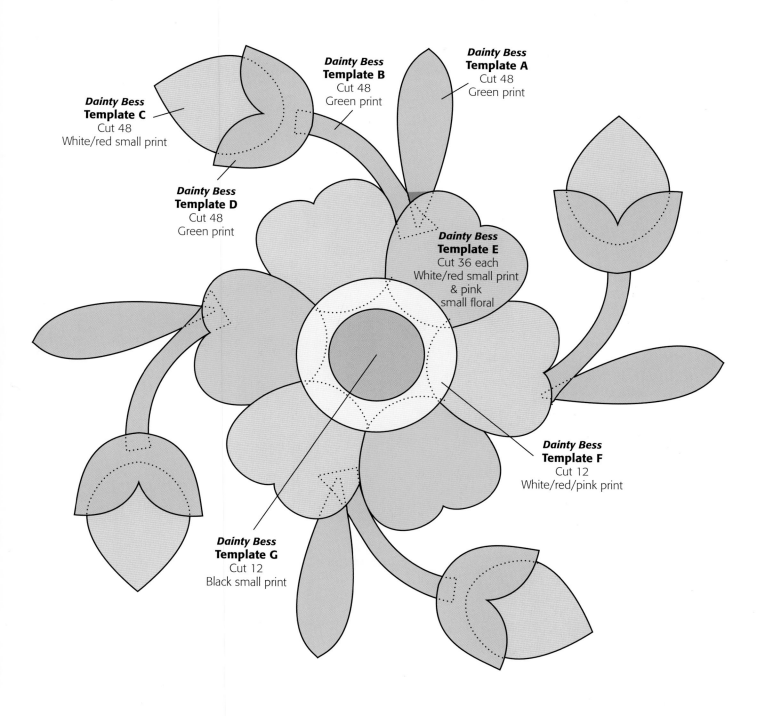

Dainty Bess
Template C
Cut 48
White/red small print

Dainty Bess
Template B
Cut 48
Green print

Dainty Bess
Template A
Cut 48
Green print

Dainty Bess
Template D
Cut 48
Green print

Dainty Bess
Template E
Cut 36 each
White/red small print
& pink
small floral

Dainty Bess
Template F
Cut 12
White/red/pink print

Dainty Bess
Template G
Cut 12
Black small print

Photographed at Old Glory Antiques, 8651 S. Gaylord Street #239, Centennial, CO 80122; 303-798-4212; oldgloryantiquesinc.com

SKILL LEVEL
INTERMEDIATE

Finished Quilt Size
41½" x 41½"

Note: Appliqué templates are printed without seam allowance.

Number of Blocks & Finished Size
9 Flower Blocks 8" x 8"

Fabric Requirements

Medium blue texture **and** white/blue print (appliqué backgrounds)	⅜ yd. **each**
#1 white print **and** blue batik (flowers)	1 fat quarter* **each**
Yellow mottle (flower centers)	5" x 5" piece
Green texture (leaves)	10" x 14" piece
Light blue print **and** light blue batik (block corners)	1 fat quarter* **each**
Assorted blue prints/textures (squares)	¾-1 yd. **total**
Assorted white/blue prints/textures (squares)	¾-1 yd. **total**
#2 white print (1st and 3rd borders)	⅝ yd.
Blue-on-blue print (binding)	⅝ yd.
Backing	2⅞ yds.
Batting size	48" x 48"

*A fat quarter is an 18" x 20-22" cut of fabric.

Blue Delft

Timeless, cheerful, and easy to incorporate into any décor…blue and white quilts never go out of style. This sweet little example is fun to make with fabrics from your stash.

Designed by
CHERYL ALMGREN TAYLOR

Machine Quilted by
CHERYL WINSLOW

Planning

Cheryl's lovely quilt was inspired by the colors of classic delftware pottery. To add interest to your version, follow Cheryl's lead and use a wide variety of blue fabrics, from light to dark, for the assorted squares in the sashing and 2nd border. Use an accurate ¼" seam allowance throughout construction, so the pieced border fits well.

Cutting Instructions
(cut in order listed)

Note: Cutting instructions for appliqué shapes are on templates.

◻ = cut in half diagonally

Medium blue texture
    5 squares 7" x 7"
White/blue print
    4 squares 7" x 7"
Light blue print
    10 squares 4⅞" x 4⅞" ◻
Light blue batik
    8 squares 4⅞" x 4⅞" ◻
Assorted blue prints/textures—
cut a total of:
    36 squares 2½" x 2½"
    18 strips 1½" x 20-22"
Assorted white/blue prints/textures—**cut a total of:**
    36 squares 2½" x 2½"
    18 strips 1½" x 20-22"
#2 white print
    *2 strips 1½" x 32½"
    *2 strips 1½" x 34½"
    **4 strips 2" x 46", pieced from 5 width of fabric (WOF) strips
Blue-on-blue print
    5 strips 2½" x WOF (binding)
*Border strips are cut to exact length.
**Border strips include extra length for trimming.

Making the Blocks

1 **Note:** Appliqué background squares are cut oversized to allow for shrinkage during appliqué. Finger-press medium blue texture 7" square in half diagonally twice; use folds as placement guide. Referring to **Diagram I-A**, position A-C in alphabetical order, keeping in mind that square will be trimmed to 6⅛" x 6⅛" (finished size is 5⅝" square). Appliqué in place. Trim to 6⅛" square. Make 5. In same manner, make and trim 4 with white/blue print background squares (**Diagram I-B**).

2 Stitch 4 light blue print half-square triangles to trimmed medium blue appliquéd square to make Flower Block (**Diagram II-A**). Make 5. In same manner, sew light blue batik triangles to white/blue appliquéd squares to make remaining 4 blocks (**Diagram II-B**).

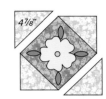

Make 5;
trim to 6⅛" square
Diagram I-A

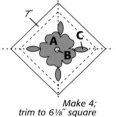

Make 4;
trim to 6⅛" square
Diagram I-B

Make 5
Diagram II-A

Make 4
Diagram II-B

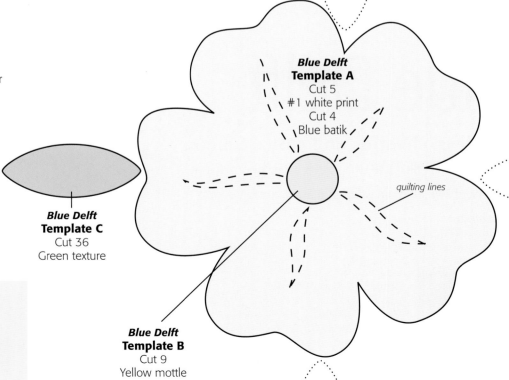

Blue Delft
Template A
Cut 5
#1 white print
Cut 4
Blue batik

quilting lines

Blue Delft
Template C
Cut 36
Green texture

Blue Delft
Template B
Cut 9
Yellow mottle

Visit
McCallsQuilting.com
to download a pattern for a lap size (54½" x 62½") version of this quilt.

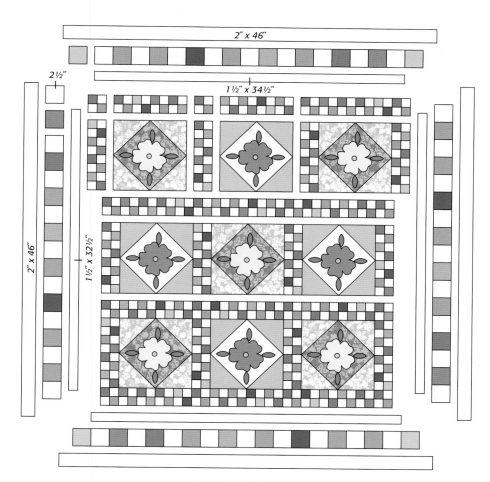

Assembly Diagram

Piecing the Sashing Units

③ Referring to **Diagram III-A**, sew together 1 each assorted blue and assorted white/blue 20-22″ strips to make strip set. Make 18 total. Press in direction of arrow. Cut into 224 segments 1½″ wide.

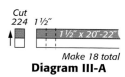

Diagram III-A

④ Sew 2 assorted segments together to make sashing post (**Diagram III-B**). Make 16 total. Sew 8 segments together to make sashing strip (**Diagrams III-C and D**). Make 12 total of each arrangement.

Make 16 total
Diagram III-B

A *Make 12 total*
Diagram III-C

B *Make 12 total*
Diagram III-D

Assembling the Quilt Top

Note: Refer to **Assembly Diagram** for following steps.

⑤ Watching placement of blue squares, stitch 4 sashing rows using 4 sashing posts and 3 sashing strips A each. Sew 3 block rows using 4 sashing strips B and 3 blocks each. Stitch rows together.

⑥ Sew #2 white print 32½″ strips to sides of quilt center. Sew #2 white 34½″ strips to top and bottom.

⑦ To make pieced border strip, stitch together 9 assorted white/blue and 8 assorted blue 2½″ squares, alternating. Make 4 total; sew 2 to sides of quilt. Stitch assorted blue 2½″ squares to ends of remaining strips; sew to top/bottom.

⑧ Sew #2 white 46″ strips to sides; trim even with top/bottom. Sew 46″ strips to top/bottom; trim even with sides.

Quilting and Finishing

⑨ Layer, baste, and quilt. Cheryl machine quilted appliqué shapes and background squares in the ditch. She added detail quilting to the flowers (see template for placement). Curved lines are quilted on block corners and small squares. The inner border is filled with a feathered vine, and the outer border with a curlicue vine. Each 2½″ square features a flower motif. Bind with blue-on-blue print.

Classic Mexican Rose

Inspired by an antique quilt, this modern version uses easy techniques to guarantee a fast yet **fabulous** finish.

Designed by
PAT SLOAN

Planning and Cutting

This charming quilt was inspired by a vintage Illinois quilt owned by Cindy Rennels. To keep things fast and easy, Pat used fusible web to do her appliqué; our instructions have you do the same. Stems are cut from a rectangle of green texture fabric prepared with fusible web. See Step 1 for instructions.

Cutting Instructions
(cut in order listed)

Note: Cutting instructions for appliqué shapes are on templates.

Green texture
  7 strips 2½" x width of fabric (WOF) for binding
  *4 strips 1½" x 44", pieced from 5 WOF strips
  1 rectangle 7" x 10"
White-on-white print
  4 squares 19½" x 19½"
  4 squares 8½" x 8½"
Red/white large floral
  *4 strips 8½" x 44", cut on lengthwise grain
*Border strips include extra length for trimming.

Appliquéing the Blocks

1 Follow manufacturer's instructions for paper-backed fusible web. Cut a 6¾" x 9¾" rectangle of fusible web; fuse to wrong side of green texture 7" x 10" rectangle, centering. From fused rectangle, cut 16 stems ⅜" x 3" and 4 stems ⅜" x 4½".

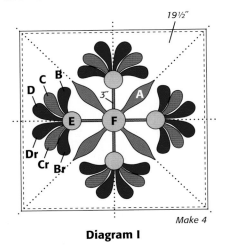

Diagram I

Make 4

2 Trace Templates A-F on paper side of fusible web. Cut apart, leaving small margin beyond drawn lines. Fuse to wrong side of appropriate fabrics; cut out on drawn lines. Finger-press white 19½" square in half on length, width, and both diagonals; use folds as placement guide. Position four 3" stems and A-F in alphabetical order (**Diagram I**). Fuse in place.

Edge-stitch using machine blanket stitch (**Diagram II**). Make 4 Four-Flower Blocks.

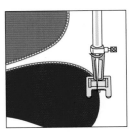

Diagram II

3 In similar manner, use white 8½" square, one 4½" stem (positioned to extend just beyond corner of square), and B-E to make One-Flower Block (**Diagram III**). Edge-stitch appliqué. **Trim** corner of stem even with white square. Make 4 One-Flower Blocks.

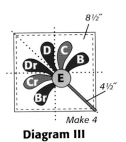

Diagram III

Make 4

Dr

Cr

Br

Classic Mexican Rose
Template D/Dr
Cut 20 each
Red texture

Classic Mexican Rose
Template C/Cr
Cut 20 each
Red floral

Classic Mexican Rose
Template B/Br
Cut 20 each
Red texture

Classic Mexican Rose
Template E
Cut 20
Gold texture

8½″ x 44″

1½″ x 44″

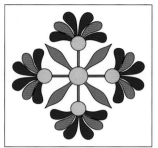

8½″ x 44″

Assembly Diagram

Assembling the Quilt Top

Note: Refer to **Assembly Diagram** for following steps.

④ Sew 2 rows of 2 blocks each. Sew rows together. Position remaining A and F shapes at center (see **photo** for placement); fuse in place. Edge-stitch appliqué.

⑤ Stitch green texture 44″ strips to sides; trim even with top and bottom. Stitch remaining green 44″ strips to top/bottom; trim even with sides.

⑥ Measure exact width of quilt center from raw edge to raw edge. Trim 2 red/white large floral 44″ strips to this measurement, and sew One-Flower Blocks to ends, watching orientation. Stitch untrimmed red/white strips to

sides; trim even with top/bottom. Stitch pieced strips to top/bottom.

Quilting and Finishing

⑦ Layer, baste, and quilt. Pat machine outline quilted the appliqué. White areas and the outer border are filled with meandering curlicues, gold circles are filled with swirls, and the green border has 2 parallel lines of quilting. Bind with green texture.

Classic Mexican Rose **Template A**
Cut 20
Green texture

Classic Mexican Rose **Template F**
Cut 5
Gold texture

Hexi-Flower Foursome

Brighten a wall with this charming tribute to all things floral. Four pretty appliquéd blocks are framed by colorful prints and easy piecing…**sew fun!**

Designed and
Machine Quilted by
JOHN KUBINIEC

SKILL LEVEL **INTERMEDIATE**

Finished Quilt Size
46½" x 46½"

Note: Appliqué templates are printed without seam allowance.

Number of Blocks and Finished Sizes
4 Appliqué Blocks 15" x 15"
69 Pieced Blocks 3" x 3"

Fabric Requirements
Yellow solid (appliqué backgrounds)   1 yd.
Green/multicolor dot (stems, leaves,
   Pieced Blocks, binding)   ⅞ yd.
Multicolor dotted stripe (pots,
   flowers, Pieced Blocks)   ⅝ yd.
Orange dotted paisley (flowers,
   Pieced Blocks, border corners)   ⅜ yd.
Assorted red/pink/orange prints
   (Pieced Blocks)   ½–¾ yd. **total**
Assorted black/purple/blue prints
   (flowers, Pieced Blocks)   ¾–1¼ yds. **total**
Yellow/white/pink floral (flowers,
   Pieced Blocks, inner border)   ⅜ yd.
Purple/fuchsia dot (outer border)   ⅝ yd.
Backing   3¼ yds.
Batting size   56" x 56"
Heat-resistant template plastic (optional)

Planning and Cutting
John chose bold prints from Rowan Fabrics to update the traditional appliqué and pieced blocks. For help making crisply turned appliqué edges, see **Preparing Hexagon Appliqués in a Snap!** (on the next page), illustrated with how-to photos.

Refer to the **Cutting Diagram** (below) when cutting the multicolor dotted stripe. Specific patches are cut from the multicolor dotted stripe and orange dotted paisley, and then these fabrics are grouped with assorted red/pink/orange prints before additional strips and appliqué flower shapes are cut.

John cut stems casually, varying the shapes for a whimsical look; do likewise if you wish. Use an accurate ¼" seam allowance throughout piecing.

1½" x 20-22"

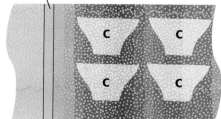

Cutting Diagram

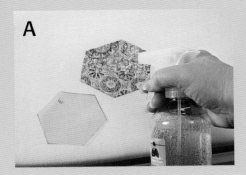

A

B

C

D

E

Preparing Hexagon Appliqués in a Snap!

Cut hexagon template shape from heat-resistant template plastic. Trace hexagon on wrong side of fabric and cut out, adding at least ¼" on all sides for turn-under allowance (it's okay if fabric shape isn't exact). Lightly spray with starch or starch alternative (**Photo A**).

Center plastic hexagon on damp fabric shape. Referring to **Photo B**, fold turn-under allowance up and over edge of plastic and press with **dry** iron (steam setting may burn your fingers).

For less bulk at points, press every other edge up first, and then press the remainder (**Photo C**).

When all edges of shape have been pressed in place, turn over and press completed shape from the right side with plastic template still in place (**Photo D**).

When cool, remove template plastic (**Photo E**) and use again.

Cutting Instructions
(cut first, and in order listed)

Note: Cutting instructions for appliqué shapes are on templates.

Yellow solid
   4 squares 16" x 16"
Green/multicolor dot
   6 strips 2½" x width of fabric (WOF) for binding
   2 strips 1½" x 20-22"
*Multicolor dotted stripe
   1 strip 1½" x 20-22"
**Orange dotted paisley
   4 squares 3½" x 3½"
Assorted red/pink/orange prints—cut a total of:**
   6 strips 1½" x 20-22"
   69 strips 1½" x 3½"
Assorted black/purple/blue prints—**cut a total of:**
   6 strips 1½" x 20-22"
   69 strips 1½" x 3½"
Yellow/white/pink floral
   ***4 strips 1" x 44", pieced from 5 WOF strips
   3 strips 1½" x 20-22"
Purple/fuchsia dot
   ***4 strips 3½" x 44", pieced from 5 WOF strips
*See **Planning and Cutting** and **Cutting Diagram.**
See **Planning and Cutting.
***Border strips include extra length for trimming.

See the video!

For a video showing how to prepare the different shapes in this quilt using this technique, visit **McCallsQuilting.com** and click on Videos, and then Partner Product Features.

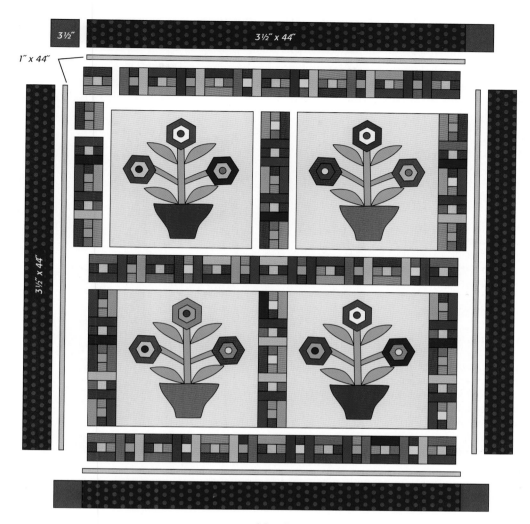

Assembly Diagram

Appliquéing and Piecing the Blocks

1 **Note:** The yellow appliqué background squares are cut oversized to allow for shrinkage during appliqué. Finger-press yellow solid 16″ square in half on both length and width; use folds as placement guide. Referring to **Diagram I**, appliqué A-G

shapes in alphabetical order. **Trim** block to 15½″ square. Make 4 total.

2 Sew together 1 each assorted black/purple/blue print, green/multicolor dot, and assorted red/pink/orange print 20-22″ strips (**Diagram II**). Press in direction of arrows. Make 2 total. Cut into 24 segments

1½″ wide. In same manner make remaining strip sets. Press and cut segments in fabric combinations and quantities shown.

3 Referring to **Diagram III**, stitch 1 each black/purple/blue and red/pink/orange 3½″ strips to sides of segment to make Pieced Block. Make 69 total.

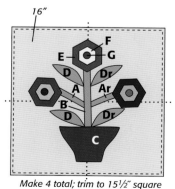

Make 4 total; trim to 15½″ square
Diagram I

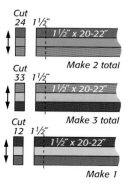

Diagram II

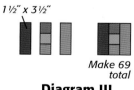

1½″ x 3½″

Make 69 total
Diagram III

Assembling the Quilt Top
Note: Refer to **Assembly Diagram** for following steps.

4 To make vertical sashing strip, stitch together 3 green-centered and 2 yellow-centered Pieced Blocks, alternating center colors and orientation (for ease in sewing). Make 6 total. Sew 2 rows using 3 vertical sashing strips and 2 Appliqué Blocks each. Sew 3 horizontal sashing rows, each using 7 yellow-centered and 6 green-centered Pieced Blocks, alternating center colors and watching orientation. Make 3 total. Sew rows together as shown.

5 Sew yellow/white/pink 44" strips to sides; trim even with top and bottom. Stitch remaining yellow strips to top/bottom; trim even with sides.

6 Measure exact width of quilt center (from raw edge to raw edge). Trim 2 purple/fuchsia dot 44" strips to this measurement and sew orange dotted paisley 3½" squares to ends. Sew remaining purple dot strips to sides; trim even with top/bottom. Add top/bottom pieced strips to quilt.

Quilting and Finishing

7 Layer, baste, and quilt. John machine quilted the appliqué and inner border in the ditch and a leaf meander in the solid yellow backgrounds. Curves are quilted in the Pieced Blocks. The outer border features wiggly lines and rows of circles stitched perpendicular to the outer edge, and the border corners are detail quilted. Bind with green/multicolor dot.

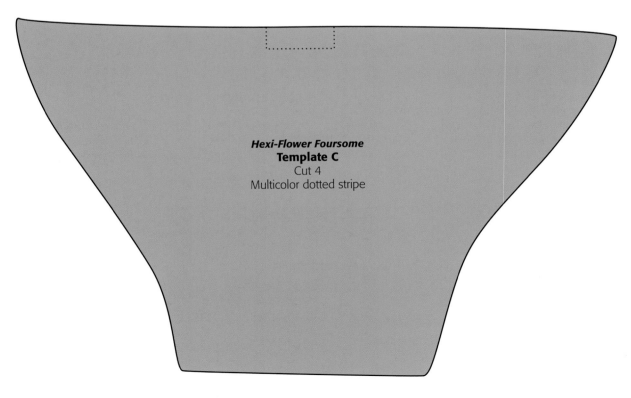

Hexi-Flower Foursome
Template C
Cut 4
Multicolor dotted stripe

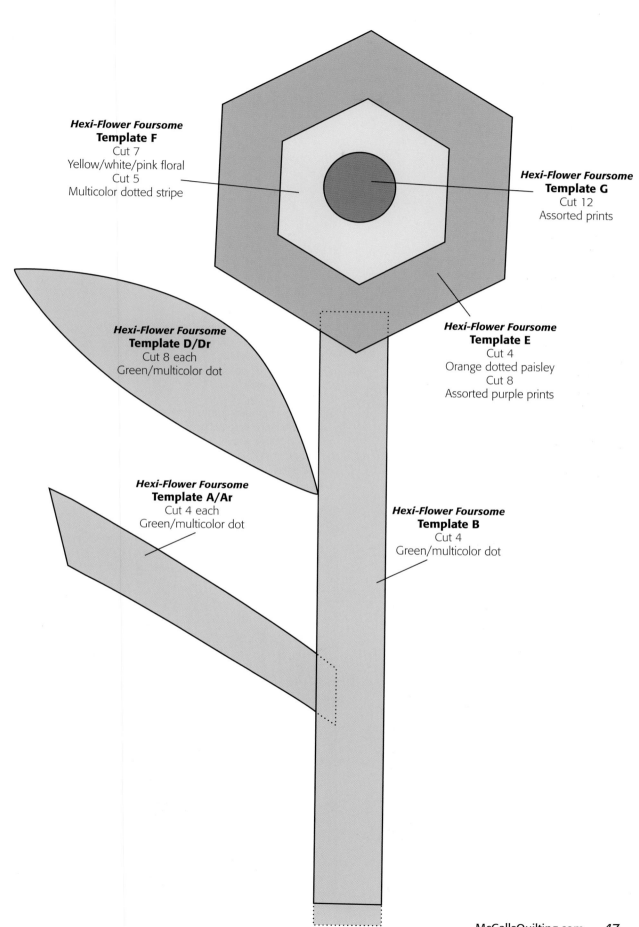

Hexi-Flower Foursome
Template F
Cut 7
Yellow/white/pink floral
Cut 5
Multicolor dotted stripe

Hexi-Flower Foursome
Template G
Cut 12
Assorted prints

Hexi-Flower Foursome
Template D/Dr
Cut 8 each
Green/multicolor dot

Hexi-Flower Foursome
Template E
Cut 4
Orange dotted paisley
Cut 8
Assorted purple prints

Hexi-Flower Foursome
Template A/Ar
Cut 4 each
Green/multicolor dot

Hexi-Flower Foursome
Template B
Cut 4
Green/multicolor dot

SKILL LEVEL **INTERMEDIATE**

Finished Quilt Size
84⅜" x 84⅜"

Number of Blocks and Finished Sizes
1 Flower Block 18" x 18"
12 Nine-Patch Blocks 10½" x 10½"

Note: Appliqué templates are printed without seam allowances, **except** bottoms of H, I/I reversed (I/Ir), K/Kr, L, and N.

Fabric Requirements

Tan print (appliqué backgrounds)	2⅛ yds.
Brown print (stems, Nine-Patch Blocks, 2nd and 4th borders)	1⅝ yds.
Red texture (flowers, binding)	1⅜ yds.
Red paisley print (flowers)	1 fat quarter*
Gold print (flower centers)	7" x 9" piece
Green print (leaves)	1 fat quarter*
Light brown print (piecing)	1⅛ yds.
Green dot (piecing)	1 yd.
Red large floral (Nine-Patch Blocks, 3rd border)	2½ yds.
Tan large floral (1st border)	2⅛ yds.
Paper-backed fusible web (optional)	2½ yds.
Backing	7⅞ yds.
Batting size	94" x 94"

*A fat quarter is an 18" x 20-22" cut of fabric.

Designed by
DOROTHY ANN WELD

Made by
KRISTI GROVE

Machine Quilted by
PAM WHIDDON

Planning

Appliqués were fused using Steam-A-Seam 2® from The Warm™ Company. If you choose to use fusible appliqué, remember to reverse shapes before tracing on paper side of fusible web.

Appliqué background **triangles** are cut to exact size for accurate piecing. The bottoms of the large-flower appliqué shapes are caught in seams during assembly for a smooth finish.

Oh, What a Beautiful Morning!

Every day should begin with something beautiful. This dramatic medallion quilt will enhance any décor, from traditional to rustic to modern.

Cutting Instructions
(cut in order listed)
Note: Cutting instructions for appliqué shapes are on templates.

◻ = cut in half diagonally

Tan print
   2 squares 24⅝" x 24⅝" ◻
   1 square 20" x 20"

Brown print
   *4 strips 2¼" x 88", pieced
      from 9 width of fabric (WOF) strips
   *4 strips 2¼" x 76", pieced from
      8 WOF strips
   1 strip 4" x WOF
   1 strip 4" x 20"

Red texture
   10 strips 2½" x WOF (binding)

Light brown print
   4 strips 4" x WOF
   8 strips 2" x 24¼"
   4 squares 3⅞" x 3⅞" ◻
   4 squares 3½" x 3½"

Green dot
   2 strips 4" x WOF
   8 strips 2" x 24¼"
   2 strips 2" x 21½"
   2 strips 2" x 18½"

Red large floral
   *4 strips 5¼" x 86", cut on
      lengthwise grain
   5 strips 4" x 40", cut on
      lengthwise grain
   2 strips 4" x 20", cut on
      lengthwise grain

Tan large floral
   *4 strips 4½" x length of fabric
      (LOF)

*Border strips include extra length for trimming.

Appliquéing and Piecing the Flower Block/Triangles

1 **Note:** The tan print background square is cut oversized to allow for shrinkage during appliqué. Finger-press tan print 20″ square in half on length, width, and both diagonals; use folds as placement guide. Referring to **Diagram I**, position A-G in alphabetical order, keeping in mind that square will be trimmed to 18½″ x 18½″ (finished size is 18″ square). Appliqué in place. **Trim** to 18½″ square, centering appliqué, to complete Flower Block.

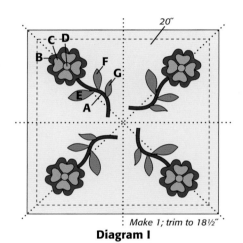

Make 1; trim to 18½″

Diagram I

2 Finger-press tan 24⅝″ half-square triangle in half (**Diagram II-A**); use fold as placement guide. Position H-N, aligning bottoms of H, I/I reversed (I/Ir), K/Kr, L, and N shapes with triangle raw edge. Appliqué in place. Make 4 flower triangles.

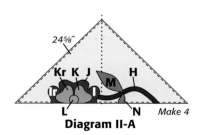

Diagram II-A

Make 4

3 Stitch together 1 each light brown print and green dot 24¼″ strips (**Diagram II-B**). Make 8 pieced strips.

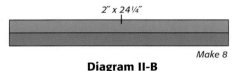

2″ x 24¼″

Diagram II-B

Make 8

4 Sew light brown 3⅞″ half-square triangle to pieced strip, watching orientation (**Diagram II-C**). Stitch to left side of flower triangle. Sew light brown 3½″ square and 3⅞″ half-square triangle to a 2nd pieced strip. Stitch to right side to complete pieced triangle. Make 4.

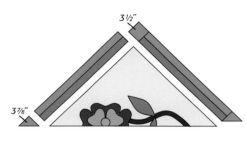

3½″

3⅞″

Diagram II-C

Make 4

Piecing the Nine-Patch Blocks

5 Referring to **Diagram III-A**, sew together 1 light brown WOF and 2 red large floral 40″ strips to make 1 strip set. Press in direction of arrows. Cut into 8 segments 4″ wide. In same manner, make remaining strip sets and cut segments shown. Sew 3 segments together to make Nine-Patch A Block (**Diagram III-B**). Make 8.

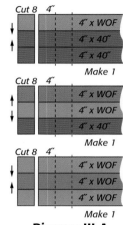

Cut 8   4″
4″ x WOF
4″ x 40″
4″ x 40″
Make 1

Cut 8   4″
4″ x WOF
4″ x WOF
4″ x 40″
Make 1

Cut 8   4″
4″ x WOF
4″ x WOF
4″ x WOF
Make 1

Diagram III-A

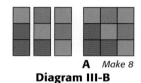

A   *Make 8*

Diagram III-B

6 In same manner, make strip sets and cut segments shown in **Diagram IV-A**. Make 4 Nine-Patch B Blocks (**Diagram IV-B**).

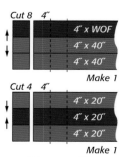

Cut 8   4″
4″ x WOF
4″ x 40″
4″ x 40″
Make 1

Cut 4   4″
4″ x 20″
4″ x 20″
4″ x 20″
Make 1

Diagram IV-A

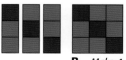

B   *Make 4*

Diagram IV-B

Assembly Diagram

Assembling the Quilt Top

Note: Refer to **Assembly Diagram** for following steps.

7 Sew green dot 18½" strips to sides of Flower Block. Sew green 21½" strips to top and bottom.

8 Watching orientation, stitch together 2 A Blocks. Make 2. Sew to sides of quilt center. Stitch together 2 B and 2 A Blocks. Make 2. Sew to top and bottom.

9 Sew pieced triangle to each side of quilt center, catching bottoms of large-flower appliqués in seams.

10 Sew tan large floral strips to sides; trim even with top/bottom. Stitch remaining tan floral strips to top/bottom; trim even with sides. In same manner, sew remaining borders to quilt, adding side strips first for each border and trimming even after each addition.

Quilting and Finishing

11 Layer, baste, and quilt. Pam machine outline quilted the appliqué, and added horizontal and vertical lines dividing the center square, and butterfly motifs on the tan triangles. Green, light brown, and brown strips are filled with continuous looping lines. Nine-Patch A Blocks are quilted with arcs and B Blocks feature flower motifs. The 1st and 3rd borders are filled with feathered vines. Bind with red texture.

See page 63 of **Basic Quiltmaking Instructions** for help with hand and machine appliqué techniques.

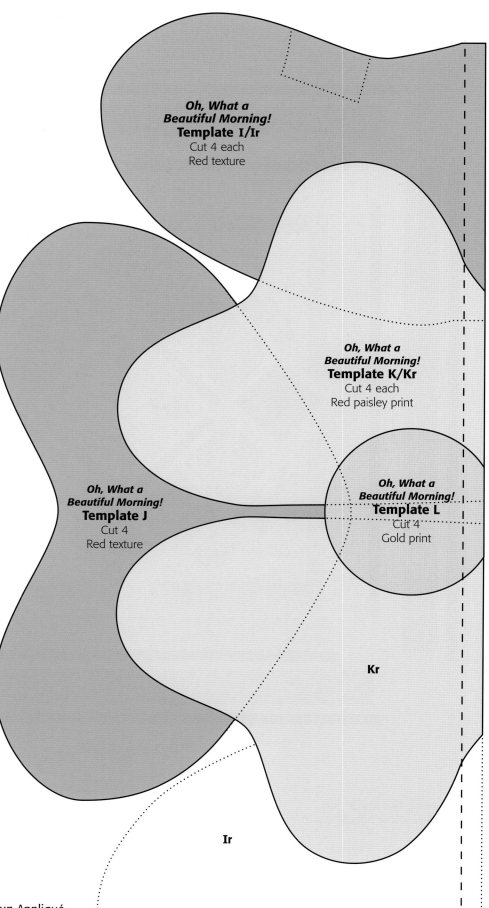

Oh, What a Beautiful Morning!
Template I/Ir
Cut 4 each
Red texture

Oh, What a Beautiful Morning!
Template K/Kr
Cut 4 each
Red paisley print

Oh, What a Beautiful Morning!
Template L
Cut 4
Gold print

Oh, What a Beautiful Morning!
Template J
Cut 4
Red texture

Kr

Ir

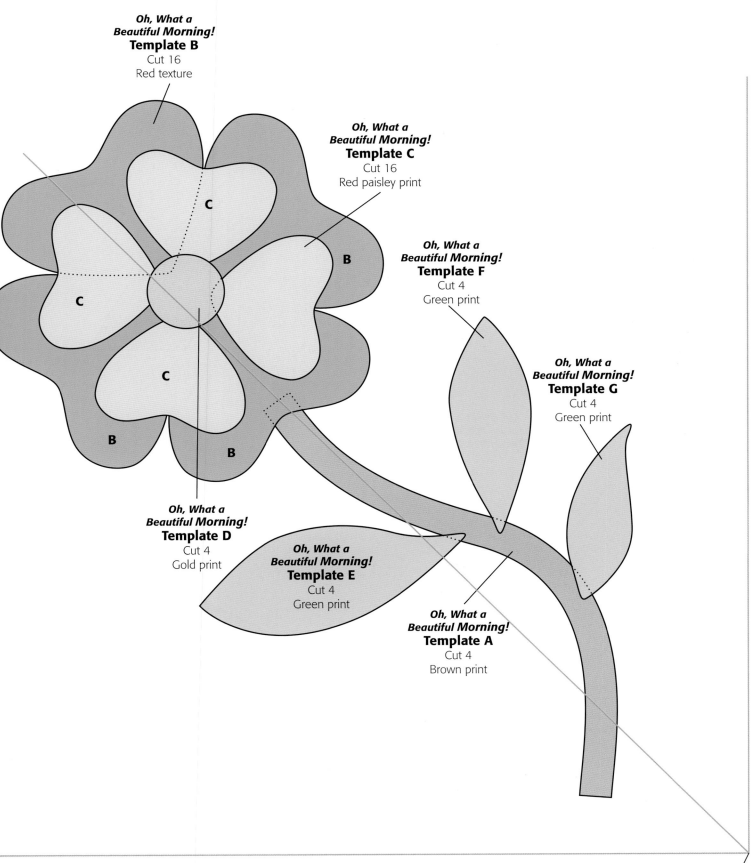

Oh, What a
Beautiful Morning!
Template B
Cut 16
Red texture

Oh, What a
Beautiful Morning!
Template C
Cut 16
Red paisley print

Oh, What a
Beautiful Morning!
Template F
Cut 4
Green print

Oh, What a
Beautiful Morning!
Template G
Cut 4
Green print

Oh, What a
Beautiful Morning!
Template D
Cut 4
Gold print

Oh, What a
Beautiful Morning!
Template E
Cut 4
Green print

Oh, What a
Beautiful Morning!
Template A
Cut 4
Brown print

C

C

C

C

B

B

B

B

Block center

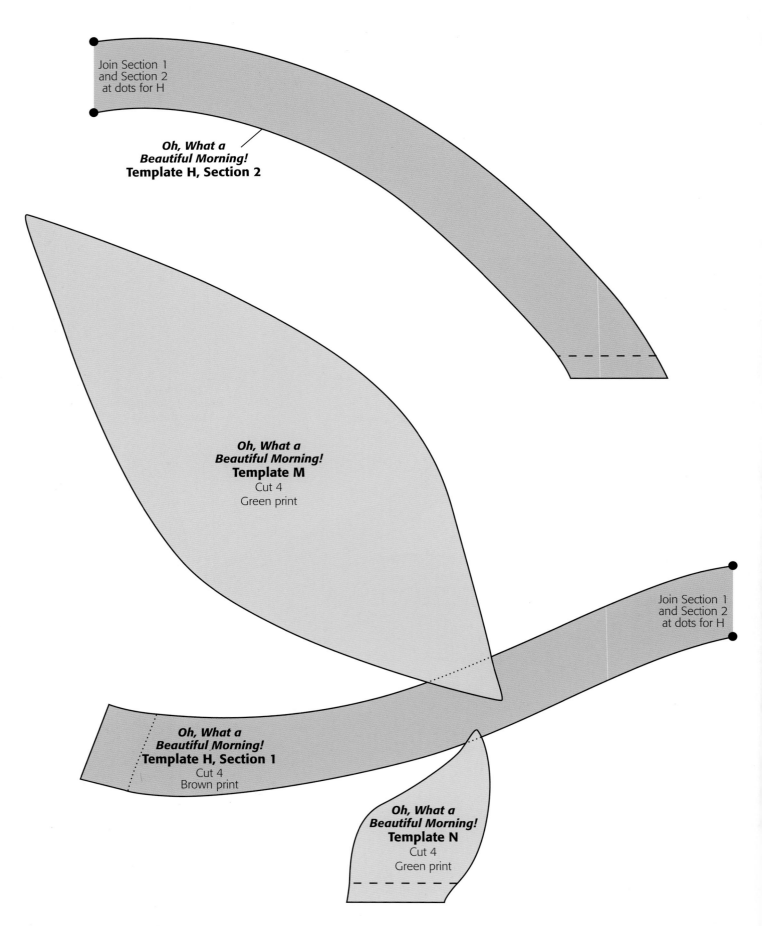

Join Section 1
and Section 2
at dots for H

*Oh, What a
Beautiful Morning!*
Template H, Section 2

*Oh, What a
Beautiful Morning!*
Template M
Cut 4
Green print

Join Section 1
and Section 2
at dots for H

*Oh, What a
Beautiful Morning!*
Template H, Section 1
Cut 4
Brown print

*Oh, What a
Beautiful Morning!*
Template N
Cut 4
Green print

Designed by
ELLIE BROWN

**SKILL LEVEL
CONFIDENT
BEGINNER**

**Finished
Banner Size**
18" x 30"

Note: Appliqué
templates are
printed without
seam allowance.

Heart of Hearts

Give someone special this quilted Valentine, and take love to a whole new dimension.

Double-sided fused hearts combine in one big heart shape, creating the unmistakable message…I ♥ U!

Fabric Requirements

White solid (background, borders, binding) — 1⅛ yds.
Fuchsia batik (pieced border) — 1 fat eighth*
Green texture (stem) — 12″ x 12″ piece
12 assorted red/fuchsia/pink batiks (hearts) — 7″ x 9″ piece each
Paper-backed fusible web — 1 yd.
Backing — ¾ yd.
Batting size — 22″ x 34″

*A fat eighth is a 9″ x 20-22″ cut of fabric.

Other Materials

Template plastic
Removable fabric marker

Planning

This cheery Valentine banner by *McCall's Quilting* art director Ellie Brown takes a fresh approach to appliqué. To make the 3-D hearts, batik squares are fused wrong sides together, hearts are cut out, and then they are machine stitched through the center onto a quilted background for a fun dimensional effect. Test removability of fabric marker on white solid before use in this project.

Cutting Instructions
(cut in order listed)

Note: Cutting instructions for appliqué shapes are in Step 4.

White solid
  3 strips 2½″ x width of fabric (binding)
  1 rectangle 12½″ x 24½″
  *2 strips 2¼″ x 30″
  *2 strips 2¼″ x 22″
  3 strips 1½″ x 20-22″
Fuchsia batik
  3 strips 1½″ x 20-22″
Green texture
  1 bias-cut strip 1″ x 15″
12 assorted red/fuchsia/pink batiks—**cut from each**:
  1 rectangle 6″ x 8″ (see Step 4)
Paper-backed fusible web
  1 strip ½″ x 15″
  6 rectangles 6″ x 8″
*Border strips include extra length for trimming.

Piecing the Background

1 Referring to **Diagram I**, sew together 1 white solid and 1 fuchsia batik 1½″ x 20-22″ strip to make strip set. Make 3. Press in direction of arrow. Cut 38 segments 1½″ wide.

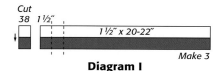

Diagram I

2 Referring to **Assembly Diagram**, sew together 12 segments. Make 2. Watching orientation, sew to sides of white

12½″ x 24½″ rectangle. Stitch together 7 segments. Make 2 and sew to top and bottom.

3 Stitch white 30″ strips to sides; trim even with top and bottom. Sew 22″ strips to top/bottom; trim even with sides.

Preparing the Appliqué and Stitching the Stem

4 Follow manufacturer's instructions for paper-backed fusible web. Center and fuse fusible web ½″ x 15″ strip to wrong side of green texture 1″ x 15″ bias-cut strip (**Diagram II**); **trim** to ¼″ x 13½″.

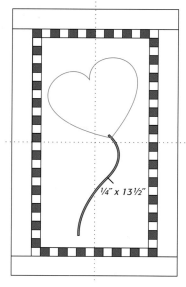

Diagram II

Fuse 6″ x 8″ fusible web rectangle to wrong side of 1 red, fuchsia, **or** pink batik rectangle. Fuse prepared rectangle to wrong side of 2nd batik rectangle to make double-sided rectangle. Make 6 total. Trace a total of 6 each Templates A and B and 24 Template C on prepared rectangles; cut out on drawn lines.

5 Finger-press banner top in half on length and width; use folds as placement guide. Trace Appliqué Placement Template on template plastic; cut out on drawn line. Referring to **Diagram III-A**, position template on quilt top and trace using removable marker. Position green bias-cut strip as shown. Fuse, taking care not to press marked heart.

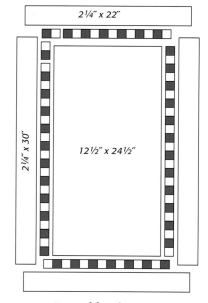

Assembly Diagram

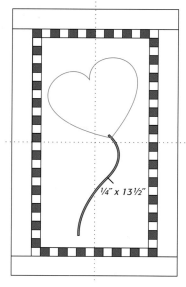

Diagram III-A

Edge-stitch stem using narrow zigzag stitch (**Diagram III-B**).

Diagram III-B

Quilting, Binding, and Completing the Appliqué

6 Layer, baste, and quilt. Ellie machine quilted a 1½″ diagonal grid across the banner using white thread. Bind with white solid.

7 Referring to **Diagram IV-A** and **banner photo**, position and pin prepared A-C within traced large heart. Straight stitch through the center of each heart through all layers, backstitching at both ends to secure (**Diagram IV-B**). To enhance 3-D effect, gently fold each heart along stitching. Following manufacturer's instructions, remove marker lines from banner front.

Diagram IV-A

Diagram IV-B

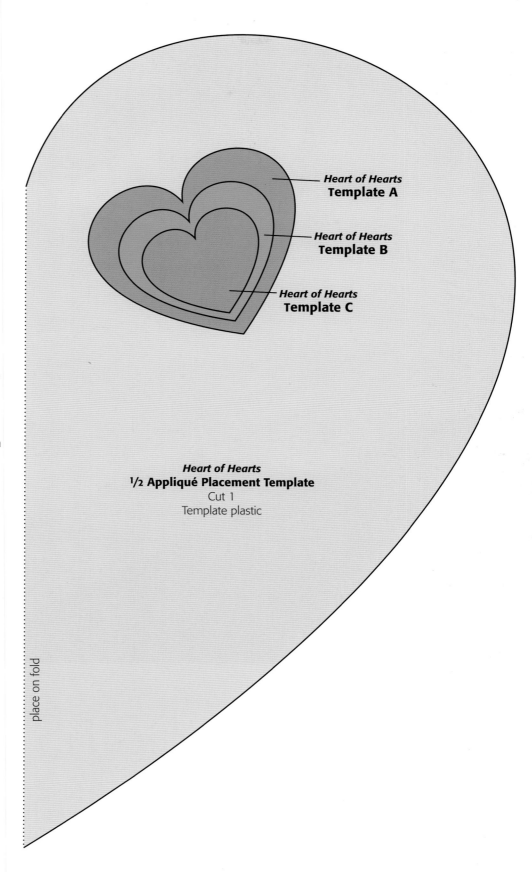

Heart of Hearts
Template A

Heart of Hearts
Template B

Heart of Hearts
Template C

Heart of Hearts
½ Appliqué Placement Template
Cut 1
Template plastic

place on fold

Daisy Chains

Bring a sweet touch of summer indoors for year-round dining pleasure. This table runner is a treat to stitch, whether you're an experienced appliqué lover or **looking to try a new skill.**

Designed and
Machine Quilted by
NANCY MAHONEY

**SKILL LEVEL
CONFIDENT BEGINNER**

**Finished Table
Runner Size**
24″ x 49″

Note: Appliqué
templates are printed
without seam allowance.

**Number of Blocks
and Finished Size**
3 Daisy Patch Blocks
12½″ x 12½″

Planning
This sweet table runner
is sure to make every
meal a special occasion!

Fabric Requirements	
Green dot (vines, leaves)	³/₈ yd.
White solid (block backgrounds, middle border)	⁵/₈ yd.*
Blue dot (petals, inner border, binding)	⁷/₈ yd.
White/blue small floral (petals)	¼ yd.
Yellow floral (flower centers)	8″ x 9″ piece
White/blue/yellow floral (outer border)	¾ yd.
Backing	1⁵/₈ yds.
Batting size	30″ x 56″
Bias bar, ¼″ (optional)	
*Yardage is based on usable width of at least 42″.	

Cutting Instructions

(cut first, and in order listed)

Note: Cutting instructions for appliqué shapes are on templates.

Green dot
    1 bias-cut strip 1" x 90" (from 1
      square 11" x 11"*)

White solid
    **2 strips 1½" x 42"
    3 squares 13½" x 13½"
    **2 strips 1½" x 19"

Blue dot
    5 strips 2½" x width of fabric (WOF)
      for binding
    **2 strips 1½" x 40"
    **2 strips 1½" x 17"

White/blue/yellow floral
    **2 strips 4" x 44", pieced from 3
      WOF strips
    **2 strips 4" x 26"

*See **How to Make Continuous Bias** in the **Basic Quiltmaking Instructions**.
**Border strips include extra length for trimming.

Appliquéing the Blocks

1️⃣ Referring to **Diagram I**, fold green dot 1" x 90" bias-cut strip in half, wrong sides together. Stitch ¼" from fold. Trim seam allowance to ⅛". Press tube flat, centering seam allowance on back so raw edge isn't visible from front. Using ¼" bias bar makes pressing faster and easier. From pressed tube, cut 12 vines each 6½" long.

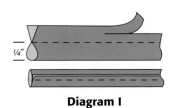

Diagram I

2️⃣ **Note:** The white appliqué background squares are cut oversized to allow for shrinkage during appliqué. Finger-press white solid 13½" square in half on both length and width and diagonally twice; use folds as placement guide. Referring to **Diagram II**, position 4 vines and A-C

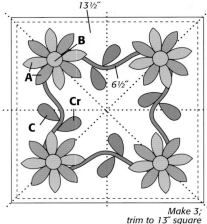

*Make 3;
trim to 13" square*

Diagram II

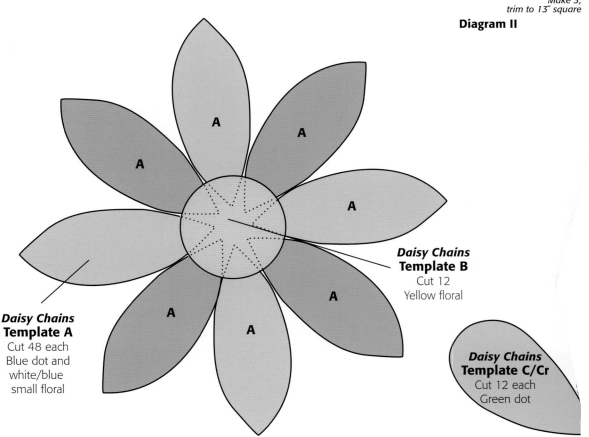

Daisy Chains
Template A
Cut 48 each
Blue dot and
white/blue
small floral

Daisy Chains
Template B
Cut 12
Yellow floral

Daisy Chains
Template C/Cr
Cut 12 each
Green dot

in alphabetical order, keeping in mind that square will be trimmed to 13″ x 13″ (finished size is 12½″ square). Appliqué in place. **Trim** to 13″ square. Make 3.

Assembling the Table Runner Top

Note: Refer to **Assembly Diagram** for following steps.

3 Sew 3 blocks together. Stitch blue dot 40″ strips to long sides; trim even with short sides. Stitch blue dot 17″ strips to short sides; trim even with long sides.

4 In same manner, sew remaining borders to quilt, adding strips to long sides first for each border and trimming even after each addition.

Quilting and Finishing

5 Layer, baste, and quilt. Nancy machine outline quilted the appliqué, and filled block backgrounds with a meander. The inner and middle borders are filled with continuous loops, and the outer border features a continuous swirl design. Bind with blue dot.

Assembly Diagram

Visit

McCallsQuilting.com...
for a pattern for a bed size (85″ x 97½″) version of this design. Click on Bonuses, and then McCall's Bonuses.

Basic Quiltmaking Instructions

All fabric requirements are based on 40"/42"-wide fabric.

The yardage given includes an additional 5% to account for fabric shrinkage and individual differences in cutting.

A ¼" seam allowance is included on pattern pieces when required.

All measurements for pieces, sashing, and borders include ¼" seam allowances.

The finished quilt size is the size of the quilt before quilting.

Because each quiltmaker usually has a personal preference, the type of batting to be used for each quilt will not be listed, unless it is necessary to obtain a specific look.

These instructions offer a brief introduction to quiltmaking. Quiltmaking instructions for projects in this issue are written for the individual with some sewing experience. Review this information if you are making your first quilt.

SUPPLIES

Scissors (for paper and template plastic)
Iron and ironing board
Marking tools: pencils, chalk markers, fine-point permanent marker (such as Pilot or Sharpie®)
Needles: package of sharps (for hand piecing) assorted sizes; package of betweens (for hand quilting), size Nos. 8 to 12
Quilting hoop or frame
Pins and pincushion
Rotary cutter and mat (at least 18" x 24")
Rulers: 2" x 18"; clear acrylic 12" square; clear acrylic 6" x 24" (for use with a rotary cutter)
Sewing machine (for machine piecing)
Shears, 8" (for fabric)
Template plastic
Thimble to fit the middle finger of your sewing hand
Thread: cotton thread or monofilament, size .004 (for machine quilting); quilting thread (for hand quilting); sewing thread in colors to match your fabrics

FABRIC PREPARATION

Pre-wash fabric to remove excess dye and minimize shrinking of completed project. Machine wash gently in warm water, dry on warm setting, and press. Immerse a swatch of fabric in a clear glass of water to test colorfastness; if dye appears, soak fabric in equal parts of white vinegar and water. Rinse and dry fabric; test another swatch. If dye still appears, do not use the fabric.

PRESSING

Proper pressing is a prerequisite for accurate piecing. Press with a light touch, using iron tip and an up and down movement. Save continuous motion "ironing" for wrinkled fabric. Use either steam or dry heat, whichever works best, and assembly-type pressing to save time.

Choose a pressing plan before beginning a project and stay consistent, if possible. Seams are "set" by first being pressed flat and then pressed either to one side, usually toward the darker fabric, or open. Sometimes, both are used in the same project, depending on the design.

To prevent distortion, press long, sewn strips widthwise and avoid raw bias edges. Other pressing hints are: use distilled water, avoid a too-hot iron which will cause fabric shininess, and pre-treat wrinkled or limp fabric with a liberal amount of spray fabric sizing.

TEMPLATES

Make templates by placing transparent plastic over the printed template pattern and tracing with a fine-point permanent marker. Trace and cut out on the stitching line (broken line) for hand-piecing templates; cut on the outer solid line for machine-piecing templates.

Label each template with the name of the quilt, template letter, grain line, and match points (dots) where sewing lines intersect. Pierce a small hole at each match point for marking match points on fabric.

FABRIC MARKING & CUTTING

Position fabric wrong side up, and place the template on the fabric. With a marker or well-sharpened pencil, trace around the template and mark match points. For hand-piecing templates, allow enough space for ¼" seam allowances to be added. For machine-piecing templates, cut along the drawn line. For hand-piecing, cut ¼" beyond the drawn line.

PIECING

Stitch fabric pieces together for patchwork by hand or machine.

Hand Piecing

Place two fabric pieces right sides together. With point of pin, match corner or other match points to align seamlines; pin. Use about an 18"-long single strand of quality sewing thread and sewing needle of your choice. To secure thread, begin at a match point and, without a knot, take a stitch and a backstitch on the seamline. Make smooth running stitches, closely and evenly spaced, stitching on the drawn line on both patches of fabric. Backstitch at the end of the seam.

How to Make Continuous Bias

1. Measure the quilt to determine how many inches of binding you need. Allow 10" extra for turning corners and the closure. Refer to chart to find the size square needed.

2. Cut the square in half diagonally (see **Diagrams A-C**). With right sides together, sew the triangles together with a ¼" seam and press open.

3. On fabric wrong side long edges, draw lines to make of your chosen binding width (see **Diagram D**). Use a c acrylic rotary ruler and a pencil or fine-point permanent p draw the lines.

4. Bring the short diagonal edges together (see **Diagrams E** F), forming a tube. Offset the drawn lines by one strip. With rig sides together, match lines with pins at the ¼" seamline and st seam; press open.

5. With scissors, cut along continuously drawn line (see **Diagram**

line. Do not stitch into the seam allowances. Press seams after the block is completed.

To join seamed pieces and strengthen the intersection, stitch through the seam allowances, and backstitch directly before and immediately after them.

Machine Piecing

Use a ¼"-wide presser foot for a seaming guide, or place a strip of opaque tape on the machine throat plate ¼" from the needle position. Place 2 fabric pieces right sides together, raw edges aligned, and pin perpendicular to the future seamline to secure. Begin and end stitching at the raw edges without backstitching; do not sew over pins. Make sure the thread tension and stitches are smooth and even on both sides of the seam. When joining seamed pieces, butt or match seams, pin to secure, and stitch. Press each seam before continuing to the next.

To chain-piece, repeatedly feed pairs of fabric pieces under the presser foot while taking a few stitches without any fabric under the needle between pairs. Cut the chained pieces apart before or after pressing.

APPLIQUÉING
Hand Appliqué

Needle-Turn Method. Place the template on the fabric right side. Draw around the template with a non-permanent marking tool of your choice, making a line no darker than necessary to be visible. Cut out the shape, including a scant ¼" seam allowance on all sides. Experience makes "eye-balling" the seam allowance quick and easy.

To blind stitch the appliqué shapes, position the appliqué shape on the background fabric, securing with a pin or a dab of glue stick. Select a sewing thread color to match the appliqué fabric. A 100% cotton thread is less visible than a cotton/polyester blend.

Begin stitching on a straight or gently curved edge, not at a sharp point or corner. Turn under a short length of seam allowance using your fingers and the point of the needle. Insert the needle into the line of the appliqué piece, coming up from the wrong side and catching just one or two threads on the edge. Push the needle through the background fabric exactly opposite the point where the thread was stitched onto the appliqué fabric piece. Coming up from the wrong side, take a stitch through the background fabric and appliqué piece, again catching just a couple threads of the appliqué fabric. Allow about ⅛" between stitches. The thread is visible on the wrong side of your block and almost invisible on the right side.

As you stitch around the edge of an appliqué fabric piece, turn under the seam allowance as you work, following the drawn line on the right side of the fabric, using your fingers and the point of the needle.

Freezer Paper Method I. Trace the template shape onto the dull side of freezer paper and cut out. With a dry iron, press the freezer paper shape, shiny side down, onto the applique fabric right side. Cut out the fabric, including a scant ¼" seam allowance on all sides. To stitch, follow the same procedure used in the Needle-Turn Method. Rather than using the drawn line as your guide, use the edge of the freezer paper.

Freezer Paper Method II. Trace the template shape onto the dull side of freezer paper and cut out. With a dry iron, press the freezer paper shape, shiny side down, onto the appliqué fabric wrong side. Cut out the fabric, including a scant ¼" seam allowance on all sides. Finger-press the seam allowance to the back of the paper template and baste in place. To stitch an appliqué fabric piece, follow the same procedure used in the Needle-Turn Method. The seam allowance has already been turned under in this technique. To remove the freezer paper, shortly before closing the appliqué, remove the basting and pluck out the freezer paper with a tweezers; or after the appliqué is sewn, cut the background fabric away behind the appliqué and remove the paper.

To reverse appliqué, two fabric pieces are layered on the background fabric, the edges of the top fabric are cut in a particular design and turned under to reveal the underlying fabric. Pin or glue the bottom appliqué fabric into position on the background block. Cut the top fabric along the specified cutting lines. Place the top fabric over the bottom fabric; check the position of the bottom fabric by holding the block up to a light source and pin. Use the Needle-Turn Method to turn under the top fabric seam allowance and appliqué, and to reveal the fabric underneath.

Machine Appliqué

Trace templates without seam allowances on paper side of paper-backed fusible web. Cut out, leaving a small margin beyond the drawn lines. Following manufacturer's instructions, apply to wrong side of appliqué fabric. Cut out on drawn line. Position appliqué on quilt where desired, and fuse to quilt following manufacturer's instructions. Finish appliqué edges by machine using a buttonhole stitch, satin stitch, or stitch of your choice.

MITERING CORNERS

Miter border corners when an angled seam complements the overall design of the quilt. Cut border strips the finished length and width of the quilt plus 4"-6" extra.

Center and pin border strips in place. Start and end seams ¼" from raw edges; backstitch to secure. Press seams away from quilt center. Lay quilt top right side up on ironing board and fold each border end flat back onto itself, right sides together, forming a 45° angle at the quilt's corner. Press to form sharp creases. Fold quilt on diagonal, right sides together. Align border strip raw edges, border seams at the ¼" backstitched point, and creases; pin in place. Stitch along crease, backstitching at ¼" border seam. Press seam open. With quilt right side up, align 45°-angle line of square ruler on seamline to check accuracy. If corner is flat and square, trim excess fabric to ¼" seam allowance.

For multiple mitered borders, sew strips together first and attach to quilt as one unit.

MARKING QUILTING PATTERNS

Press quilt top and change any correctable irregularities. Choose a marking

	2"-Wide Bias Strip	2½"-Wide Bias Strip	3"-Wide Bias Strip
	16" square	18" square	20" square
	23" square	26" square	28" square
	28" square	32" square	35" square
	33" square	37" square	40" square

UARE TO CUT

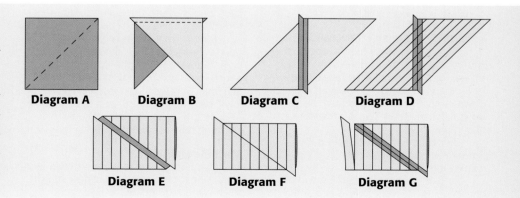

Diagram A   Diagram B   Diagram C   Diagram D

Diagram E   Diagram F   Diagram G

tool which makes a thin accurate line, and pre-test removability on quilt fabric scraps.

Marking tool options include: water-soluble and air-erasable markers, white dressmaker's pencil, chalk pencils, chalk rolling markers, and slivers of hardened soap. Try silver and yellow Berol® pencils on dark fabrics and a No. 2 pencil sparingly on light fabric. The same project may need several types of markers.

Design aid options include: freezer-paper cutouts, stencils, templates, household items such as cookie cutters, and acrylic rulers.

After marking quilting designs of choice, do not press quilt top; markings could be set permanently.

BACKING

Use the same quality backing fabric as used in the quilt top. Remove selvages and cut backing at least 4" larger than quilt top on all sides. It is necessary to seam backing for quilts larger than 36" wide when using standard 44"/45"-wide fabric. Use either vertical or horizontal seaming, whichever requires less fabric. Press backing seams open.

BATTING

Standard pre-cut batting sizes are:

Crib	45" x 60"
Twin	72" x 90"
Double	81" x 96"
Queen	90" x 108"
King	120" x 120"

Consider several factors when choosing batting. How do you want the quilt to look? How close will the quilting stitches be? Are you hand or machine quilting? How will the quilt be used?

Batting is made from different fibers (not all fibers are available in all sizes). If you prefer an old-fashioned looking quilt, consider using a mostly cotton batting. The newer cotton battings are bonded and do not require the close quilting that old-fashioned cotton battings once did. If you don't want to do a lot of quilting, use a regular or low-loft polyester batting. If you like "puffy" quilts, use a high-loft polyester batting. Wool battings are also available.

If you are not sure which batting is right for your project, consult the professionals at your local quilt shop.

LAYERING THE QUILT SANDWICH

Mark the center of the backing on the wrong side at the top, bottom, and side edges. On a smooth, flat surface a little larger than the quilt, place backing right side down. Smooth any wrinkles until the backing is flat; use masking tape to hold it taut and in place.

Unfold batting and lay over backing. Smooth wrinkles, keeping the backing wrinkle free.

Position quilt top on backing and batting, keeping all layers wrinkle free. Match centers of quilt top with backing. Use straight pins to keep layers from shifting while basting.

BASTING

Basting holds the three layers together to prevent shifting while quilting.

For hand quilting, baste using a long needle threaded with as long a length of sewing thread as can be used without tangling. Insert needle through all layers in center of quilt and baste layers together with a long running stitch. For the first line of basting, stitch up and down the vertical center of the quilt. Next, baste across the horizontal center of the quilt. Working toward the edges and creating a grid, continue basting to completely stabilize the layers.

For machine quilting, pin-baste using nickel-plated safety pins, instead of needle and thread. Begin in the center of the quilt and work outward to the edges, placing safety pins approximately every 4".

QUILTING
Hand Quilting

Hand quilting features evenly spaced, small stitches on both sides of the quilt with no knots showing on the back.

Most quilters favor 100% cotton thread in ecru or white, though beautiful colors are available.

Beginners start with a size 8 or 9 "between" needle and advance to a shorter, finer size 10 or 12 needle for finer stitching. Use a well-fitting, puncture-proof thimble on the middle finger of your sewing hand to position and push the needle through the quilt layers.

A frame or hoop keeps the layered quilt smooth and taut; choose from a variety of shapes and sizes. Select a comfortable seat with proper back support and a good light source, preferably natural light, to reduce eye strain.

To begin, cut thread 24" long and make a knot on one end. Place the needle tip either into a seamline or ½" behind the point where quilting stitches are to begin and guide it through the batting and up through the quilt top to "bury" the knot. Gently pull on the thread until you hear the knot "pop" through the quilt top. Trim the thread tail.

To quilt using a running stitch, hold the needle parallel to the quilt top and stitch up and down through the three layers with a rocking motion, making several stitches at a time. This technique is called stacking. Gently and smoothly pull the thread through the layers. To end, make a small knot and bury it in the batting.

Machine Quilting

Machine quilting requires an even-feed or walking foot to ensure quilting a straight stitch without distorting the layers, and a darning foot for free-motion or heavily curved stitching.

Use 100% cotton thread or size .004 monofilament thread (clear for light-colored fabrics, smoky for dark fabrics) on the top and cotton in the bobbin. Pre-test stitch length and thread tension using two muslin pieces layered with batting. Adjust as needed.

Choose a quilting strategy. Begin stitching in the middle and work outward, making sure the layers are taut. Roll the edges of the quilt compactly to reveal the area being quilted; reroll as needed. To secure the thread, take 1 or 2 regular-length stitches forward, backward, and continue forward; stitch a few very small stitches and gradually increase to desired length. Trim thread tails.

Stitch "in the ditch" or along the seamline to secure quilt layers while adding subtle texture. Stitch open areas with a design of your choice.

MAKING BINDING STRIPS

Quilt binding can be cut on the bias or straight of grain. Use a continuous strip of bias for a quilt that will be used frequently or has scalloped edges and rounded corners. Refer to "How To Make Continuous Bias" on pages 62 and 63 for making continuous bias binding. For bias or straight-grain double-fold binding, cut 2½"- or 3"-wide strips of fabric and fold in half, wrong sides together.

ATTACHING THE BINDING

Beginning near the middle of any side, align binding and quilt raw edges. Sew to the corner and stop stitching ¼" from the quilt edge; backstitch to secure (an even-feed foot is very helpful). Remove from sewing machine. Fold the binding strip up and back down over itself, aligning raw edges on the second side, and pin in place. Beginning ¼" from the quilt edge (same point where stitching stopped on the first side), sew binding to second side and stop stitching ¼" from next corner edge; backstitch. Remove from sewing machine and continue in the same manner. After sewing all sides, finish using the technique of choice. Wrap binding around to the back side, using your fingers to manipulate corner to achieve a miter on both front and back sides. Pin and blindstitch in place.

SIGNING YOUR QUILT

You will want to sign and date your quilt and record other information important to you, such as the quilt's name, your city and state, and the event the quilt commemorates. You may embroider or use permanent ink to record this information on a piece of fabric that you then stitch to the quilt backing, or you may embroider directly on the quilt.